DATE DUE

UNDERSTANDING DRUGS

Hallucinogens

TITLES IN THE *UNDERSTANDING DRUGS* SERIES

UNDERSTANDING DRUGS

DRUGS

Hallucinogens

THOMAS SANTELLA

CONSULTING EDITOR:
DAVID J. TRIGGLE
University Professor
School of Pharmacy and Pharmaceutical Sciences
State University of New York at Buffalo

CHELSEA HOUSE
An Infobase Learning Company

Chelsea House
An Infobase Learning Company
132 West 31st Street
New York NY 10001

Library of Congress Cataloging-in-Publication Data

Santella, Thomas M.
  Hallucinogens / Thomas Santella ; consulting editor David J. Triggle.
    p. cm. — (Understanding drugs)
  Includes bibliographical references and index.
  ISBN-13: 978-1-60413-539-8 (hardcover : alk. paper)
  ISBN-10: 1-60413-539-5 (hardcover : alk. paper)   1. Hallucinogenic drugs.
I. Triggle, D. J. II. Title. III. Series.
  RM324.8.S26 2012
  615.7'883—dc23

                                                                2011029244

Chelsea House books are available at special discounts when purchased in bulk quantities for businesses, associations, institutions, or sales promotions. Please call our Special Sales Department in New York at (212) 967-8800 or (800) 322-8755.

You can find Infobase Learning on the World Wide Web at
http://www.infobaselearning.com

Text design by Kerry Casey
Cover design by Alicia Post
Composition by Newgen North America
Cover printed by IBT Global, Troy, N.Y.
Book printed and bound by IBT Global, Troy, N.Y.
Date printed: December 2011
Printed in the United States of America

10 9 8 7 6 5 4 3 2 1

This book is printed on acid-free paper.

All links and Web addresses were checked and verified to be correct at the time of publication. Because of the dynamic nature of the Web, some addresses and links may have changed since publication and may no longer be valid.

Contents

foreword

THE USE AND ABUSE OF DRUGS

For thousands of years, humans have used a variety of sources with which to cure their ills, cast out devils, promote their well-being, relieve their misery, and control their fertility. Until the beginning of the twentieth century, the agents used were all of natural origin, including many derived from plants as well as elements such as antimony, sulfur, mercury, and arsenic. The sixteenth-century alchemist and physician Paracelsus used mercury and arsenic in his treatment of syphilis, worms, and other diseases that were common at that time; his cure rates, however, remain unknown. Many drugs used today have their origins in natural products. Antimony derivatives, for example, are used in the treatment of the nasty tropical disease leishmaniasis. These plant-derived products represent molecules that have been "forged in the crucible of evolution" and continue to supply the scientist with molecular scaffolds for new drug development.

Our story of modern drug discovery may be considered to start with the German physician and scientist Paul Ehrlich, often called the father of chemotherapy. Born in 1854, Ehrlich became interested in the ways in which synthetic dyes, then becoming a major product of the German fine chemical industry, could selectively stain certain tissues and components of cells. He reasoned that such dyes might form the basis for drugs that could interact selectively with diseased or foreign cells and organisms. One of Ehrlich's early successes was development of the arsenical "606"—patented under the name *Salvarsan*—as a treatment for syphilis. Ehrlich's goal was to create a "magic bullet," a drug that would target only the diseased cell or the invading disease-causing organism and have no effect on healthy cells and tissues. In this he was not successful, but his great research did lay the groundwork for the successes of the twentieth century, including the discovery of the sulfonamides and the antibiotic penicillin. The latter agent saved countless lives during World War II. Ehrlich, like many scientists, was an optimist. On the eve of World War I, he wrote, "Now that the liability to, and danger of, disease are to a large extent circumscribed—the efforts of chemotherapeutics are directed as far as possible to fill up the gaps left in this ring." As we shall see in the pages of this volume, it is neither the first nor the last time that science has proclaimed its victory over nature, only to have to see this optimism dashed in the light of some freshly emerging infection.

From these advances, however, has come the vast array of drugs that are available to the modern physician. We are increasingly close to Ehrlich's magic bullet: Drugs can now target very specific molecular defects in a number of cancers, and doctors today have the ability to investigate the human genome to more effectively match the drug and the patient. In the next one to two decades, it is almost certain that the cost of "reading" an individual genome will be sufficiently cheap that, at least in the developed world, such personalized medicines will become the norm. The development of such drugs, however, is extremely costly and raises significant social issues, including equity in the delivery of medical treatment.

The twenty-first century will continue to produce major advances in medicines and medicine delivery. Nature is, however, a resilient foe. Diseases and organisms develop resistance to existing drugs, and new drugs must constantly be developed. (This is particularly true for anti-infective and anticancer agents.) Additionally, new and more lethal forms of existing infectious diseases can develop rapidly. With the ease of global travel, these can spread from Timbuktu to Toledo in less than 24 hours and become pandemics. Hence the current concerns with avian flu. Also, diseases that have previously been dormant or geographically circumscribed may suddenly break out worldwide. (Imagine, for example, a worldwide pandemic of Ebola disease, with public health agencies totally overwhelmed.) Finally, there are serious concerns regarding the possibility of man-made epidemics occurring through the deliberate or accidental spread of disease agents—including manufactured agents, such as smallpox with enhanced lethality. It is therefore imperative that the search for new medicines continue.

All of us at some time in our life will take a medicine, even if it is only aspirin for a headache or to reduce cosmetic defects. For some individuals, drug use will be constant throughout life. As we age, we will likely be exposed to a variety of medications—from childhood vaccines to drugs to relieve pain caused by a terminal disease. It is not easy to get accurate and understandable information about the drugs that we consume to treat diseases and disorders. There are, of course, highly specialized volumes aimed at medical or scientific professionals. These, however, demand a sophisticated knowledge base and experience to be comprehended. Advertising on television is widely available but provides only fleeting information, usually about only a single drug and designed to market rather than inform. The intent of this series of books, **Understanding Drugs**, is to provide the lay reader with intelligent, readable, and accurate descriptions of drugs, why and how they are used, their limitations, their side effects and their future. The series will discuss both *"treatment drugs"*—typically, but not exclusively, prescription drugs, that have well-established criteria of both efficacy and safety—and *"drugs of abuse"* that have pronounced pharmacological and physiological effects but that are considered, for a variety of reasons, not to be considered for therapeutic purposes. It is our hope that these books will provide readers with sufficient information to satisfy their immediate needs and to serve as an adequate base for further investigation and for asking intelligent questions of health care providers.

—David J. Triggle, Ph.D.
University Professor
School of Pharmacy and Pharmaceutical Sciences
State University of New York at Buffalo

1
An Introduction to Hallucinogens

Ben had made it halfway through his first semester at New York University. Adjusting to life at a new school and trying to develop a new group of friends, not to mention learning his way around New York City, was indeed taking its toll on Ben's stress level. A talented piano player, Ben met a few other musically inclined students early on and in short order they formed a band and met every Friday evening to practice.

It was after one of the band's rehearsals that the topic of trying LSD first came up. Kelly, the saxophonist in the group, had met a guy who could sell them a few tabs of the psychedelic substance, "super cheap," she said. She'd never tried it, nor had any of the other band members for that matter, but they'd all been reading Aldous Huxley's The Doors of Perception *in their Intro to Modern American Lit class, and it had certainly ignited their interest. The book was essentially about the author's own experience using mescaline, a drug similar to LSD, but found in the naturally occurring peyote plant. Unaware of the consequences of the decision they were about to make, the band—Ben, Kelly, Jeff, Ed (the drummer), and Debbie (the bass player)—decided that they would try LSD together. They agreed it would be a fun little "experiment." By the next Friday practice, Kelly, just as she'd indicated the previous week, had gotten hold of five hits of acid.*

Kelly handed out to her band mates the tabs of acid, each on a tiny sheet of paper material with a half-moon printed on it. There was a palpable sense of nervousness in the room, and what had been a loud and raucous evening in the warehouse practice space quickly fell into an eerie silence. Just then Ed, who was normally quiet but especially so tonight, broke his, as well as the group's, silence.

"I think I'm gonna sit out on this one guys," Ed said, handing the innocent-looking drug back to Kelly.

"Really?" she said, "That's pretty lame. You know we're young, right? And freshmen in college? We're supposed to try new things. I mean, don't you want to have new experiences?"

"I guess," Ed replied, "But how do you know what's in that? I mean, it could be anything. How do you know it's good? How do you know if it's safe?"

"Well, I guess I don't," Kelly said, clearly a little taken back by Ed's reasoning. "It could be dangerous I suppose," she said, regaining her poise, "but that's part of the fun, right?"

"No offense," Ed said, "but I'm just not willing to put my life on the line like this, ingesting some chemicals prepared by . . . well, who even knows where it came from, or who made it."

"Your decision," Kelly said, popping the tab into her mouth. Jeff and Ben quickly followed suit. Debbie appeared to have taken the hit just like the others, but Ed's cautionary words scared her a little, and she actually just pretended to take the drug while sliding it instead into her pocket.

For thousands of years, people have taken naturally occurring hallucinogens for various reasons. Different cultures have used the drugs to induce "visions" or dreams that have been thought to provide mystical foresight, fortune-telling, or special powers; some communities continue those practices today. In a general sense, however, the use of these mind-altering substances decreased in the modern era, as the emergence of the Abrahamic religions (Judaism, Christianity, Islam) placed greater emphasis on the priesthood, as opposed to direct spiritual experience, a purpose for which these drugs were often used.

In the mid-20th century, however, people started using synthetic hallucinogens, such as d-lysergic acid diethylamide, commonly known as LSD, purely for recreational purposes, specifically in Western societies such as the United States. The use of these drugs, referred to collectively as psychedelics, exploded in the 1960s, as a burgeoning countercultural youth movement emerged. Commonly associated with psychedelic rock, artists, pop figures, and their followers, often described as "hippies," a new culture based principally on hallucinogens like LSD, peyote, and "magic mushrooms" took

Figure 1.1 Peyote plants, which contain mescaline, growing in the wild. (© *shutterstock*)

root. Personalities such as influential American psychologist and psychedelic enthusiast Timothy Leary and writer Aldous Huxley brought debate over the legitimate use of these substances into the mainstream. In short order, however, the use of psychedelics took on a negative persona across the country, and their users were seen as pariahs within mainstream culture.[1]

Perhaps burnt out on the effects of these intense and unpredictable drugs, or perhaps replaced by other substances like cocaine and **heroin** in the 1970s, the use of hallucinogens declined in the ensuing decades. In more recent years, though, specifically the 1990s, the use of hallucinogens began to rise again, a trend that continues today.

WHAT ARE HALLUCINOGENS?

Hallucinogens are drugs that cause profound distortions in a user's perceptions of reality. Users often see images, hear sounds, and feel sensations that seem real but do not exist. Some hallucinogens produce rapid, intense mood swings. Hallucinogens initiate their effects by disrupting the interaction of nerve cells and the neurotransmitter **serotonin.** The most common hallucinogens are LSD; paramethoxyamphetamine (PMA); 4-bromo-2, 5-dimethoxyhenethylamine (2 C-B); peyote; and certain varieties of mushrooms.[2]

While there are many different drugs, both naturally occurring and synthetically produced, that are considered hallucinogens, they are generally divided into three distinct categories—psychedelics, dissociatives, and deliriants.

Psychedelics

The most common subset of the hallucinogens, the term *psychedelic* was coined by psychiatric researcher Dr. Humphry Osmond to describe drugs that "catalyze the emergence into conscious awareness of previously unconscious, subconscious, repressed, or filtered cognitions."[3] Put another way, these substances cause the user to experience dream-like sensations that dramatically alter one's perceptions. Many users describe intensified sensations of taste, color, smell, and sound. The term *psychedelic* typically refers to LSD; psilocybin (mushrooms); mescaline; ibogaine; 3,4-methylenedioxymethamphetamine (MDMA); and dimethyltryptamine (**DMT**).[4]

Dissociatives

Dissociatives are a group of hallucinogens, initially developed as general anesthetics for surgery. Rather than amplify sensations, dissociatives produce feelings of detachment from the environment and self—a kind of sensory deprivation. The primary dissociatives are **phencyclidine** (PCP, angel dust), **ketamine,** DXM (**dextromethorphan,** an active ingredient in many cough syrups), and nitrous oxide, among others. These substances cause the user to feel emotionless, detached from any pain.[5]

Deliriants

Finally, deliriants are the least popular and least commonly used substances within the hallucinogen class. This is the result of the extreme side effects produced by these drugs, which are mostly derived directly from plants. As the name suggests, deliriants cause extreme confusion, agitation, and lack of coordination. Unlike many psychedelics and dissociatives, deliriants are toxic

DO HALLUCINOGENS CAUSE HALLUCINATIONS?

An interesting debate about hallucinogens is whether or not they in fact actually cause hallucinations. According to Dictionary.com, a hallucination is "a sensory experience of something that does not exist outside the mind, caused by various physical and mental disorders, or by reaction to certain toxic substances, and usually manifested as visual or auditory images." Like this definition, most others include references to toxic substances (e.g., psychedelic drugs) in their definition of a hallucination. Nevertheless, many experts indicate that there is a subtle difference between the experience of using hallucinogens and actual hallucinations. The difference, they say, is that in a true hallucination, one does not recognize that one is hallucinating. In other words, one completely believes the imaginary experience is real. Alternatively, experts report that users of hallucinogens, at least at typical dosages, have similar sensory, "hallucinogenic" experiences, but realize that the experience is not actually real.

at high levels, causing life-threatening physical reactions. The most common deliriants include deadly nightshade, mandrake, henbane, and datura. Deliriants also cause hallucination in the true sense, where the user is not conscious of the effects of the drug. The experience is similar to sleepwalking, in that the user does not remember the experience.[6]

KEY HEALTH ISSUES

While the intensity of a hallucinogen's effects may differ, depending on type of drug, dose, and the user's own hereditary characteristics (e.g., natural levels of serotonin in the brain), hallucinogens produce several common physical symptoms: dilated pupils, raised body temperature, increased heart rate and blood pressure, profuse sweating, loss of appetite, ataxia (uncoordinated movements), sleeplessness, dry mouth, and tremors. In the case of mescaline (the active ingredient in peyote), when used by pregnant women, fetal abnormalities have been reported.[7]

Despite much serious research, relatively little is known about the long-term health effects of hallucinogens. Experts generally agree that there are very few long-term effects, or permanent brain damage, associated with hallucinogen use. It is also understood that these drugs are not addictive in the way that other substances are, such as heroin, cocaine, or nicotine, for example. Moreover, users do not tend to become tolerant of these drugs, thus they do not increase dosages over time. In fact, typically users often need time to recover from the use of a hallucinogen, and thus do not take these drugs multiple times in a day or even week.

The fact that limited fatal health effects occur directly from using hallucinogens does not mean that these drugs are not dangerous. Most of the danger associated with hallucinogens comes from the user's often irrational actions while under the influence. Cases of suicide, death from high falls,

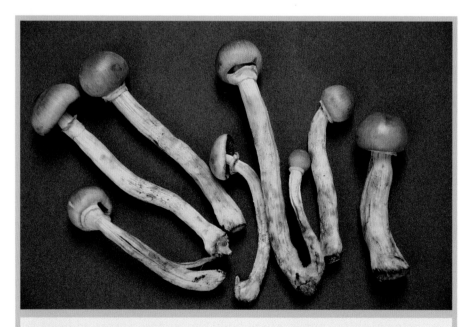

Figure 1.2 Psychoactive mushrooms can cause visual hallucinations, mood changes, paranoia, and confusion. *(Alamy)*

hypothermia, and many other fatal accidents have been associated with the use of these substances. In addition, the long-term use of hallucinogens has, in some cases, resulted in permanent psychiatric problems and adverse mental conditions.

LEGAL ISSUES

The laws controlling and prohibiting hallucinogens have been debated since the government began passing them. As of 2008, most well-known hallucinogens (aside from dextromethorphan and **dimenhydrinate**) are illegal in most Western countries. Hallucinogens are relatively inexpensive, domestically produced, and not part of a network of distributors battling over markets or territory. That said, the legal repercussions in the United States for the possession for hallucinogens are on par with other illegal drugs.

While there are exceptions for some naturally occurring hallucinogens, and also exceptions for certain religious groups who use hallucinogens in religious ceremonies, the majority of these substances are illegal in the United States. Practically speaking, this means that there are stiff penalties for selling, purchasing, and using these drugs.

Hallucinogens like LSD and MDMA have not always been classified as illegal products. In fact, it wasn't until 1970, with the creation of the Controlled Substances Act (CSA), that hallucinogens were classified as Schedule I controlled substances. This meant that the government viewed these drugs as dangerous, even under medical supervision, with no medical benefit. As a result, the use, possession, and distribution of these hallucinogens came under the criminal code.

Recently, a growing group of opponents of the Schedule I classification have called for a re-evaluation of these drugs. These critics argue that, as the Drug Enforcement Agency (DEA) recognizes, hallucinogens are not addictive and therefore are not abused in the same way as other Schedule I drugs, such as cocaine and heroin. To date, however, the government, specifically the DEA, maintains that the Schedule I classification is correct. It argues that relaxing the classification and thus easing penalties would only result in more use. Proponents of the classification argue that, while these substances may not be addictive, they are "gateway" drugs, meaning that they often lead to the use of other more addictive drugs.

One exception, when it comes to the illegal classification of hallucinogens, is peyote. In the 1930s, when the limitations on hallucinogens, including peyote, were first implemented, certain Native American tribes protested strongly. They argued that peyote was a part of their religious existence and had been for many generations. As such, they utilized the First and Fourteenth amendments of the U.S. Constitution to argue that this was an issue of religious freedom. The court agreed and, to date, several Native American tribes are legally allowed to use peyote, even though it remains a Schedule I controlled substance under the U.S. drug code.

In the end, when it comes to the legal status of hallucinogens, there is typically a single question posed: Does the government have the right to prohibit its citizenry from using these substances; or, should the individual have the right to decide for him or herself, whether the use of hallucinogens is appropriate? Indeed there are persuasive arguments on both sides of this question. Clearly, part of the government's job is to protect its citizenry, whether from war, disease, or other threats. Many view drug use, especially when it rises to

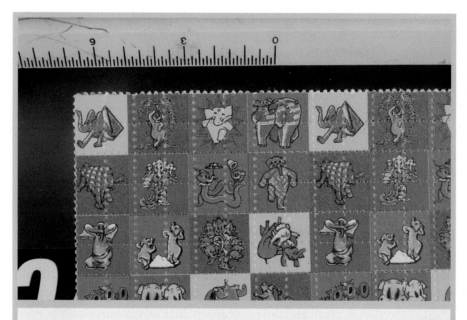

Figure 1.3 The most common form of LSD is "blotter acid," sheets of paper soaked in the drug and sold in perforated individual dosage units. *(Drug Enforcement Administration)*

the level of abuse, as a legitimate threat, which the government has the right to protect against. And yet the use of hallucinogens continues today, as it has for many generations.

THE USE AND ABUSE OF HALLUCINOGENS

Hallucinogen *dependence* is generally defined as the continued use of hallucinogens, even when the substances cause the affected individual significant problems, or when the user knows of adverse effects (memory impairment while intoxicated, anxiety attacks, flashbacks), but continues to use the substances anyway. "Craving" hallucinogens after not using them for a period of time has been reported. Hallucinogen *abuse* is repeated use of hallucinogens, even after they have caused the user impairment that undermines his ability to fulfill obligations at work, school, or at home. Hallucinogens distort and intensify auditory and visual sensations. For example, users may feel as if they are seeing sounds and hearing colors. People feel as if they are not real (called **depersonalization**) or are detached from their environment (called dissociation). Many hallucinogens cause nausea and vomiting. LSD causes blurred vision, sweating, palpitations, and impaired coordination. The actual effect can depend on the user's mood, the user's expectations of the substance, as well as the setting in which the drug is taken.

In terms of use, the 1960s and early 1970s were the high-water mark for consumption of hallucinogens in the United States. Whether as a result of real

Table 1.1 LSD Use by U.S. Students, 2008			
	8th Grade	**10th Grade**	**12th Grade**
Lifetime	1.9%	2.6%	4.0%
Past Year	1.3%	1.8%	2.7%
Past Month	0.5%	0.7%	1.1%

Note: "Lifetime" refers to use at least once during a respondent's lifetime. "Past year" refers to use at least once during the year preceding an individual's response to the survey. "Past month" refers to use at least once during the 30 days preceding an individual's response to the survey.
Source: National Institute on Drug Abuse, 2008 Monitoring the Future Survey, http://www.monitoringthefuture.org/pubs/monographs/vol1_2008.pdf.

or perceived hazards, the use of hallucinogens actually declined in the 1980s, only to resurge in the 1990s. According to the DEA, in 1999, "one out of every six college students (14.8%) reported some use of hallucinogens in their lifetime."[8] Today hallucinogens remain popular among college, high school, and even junior high school students.

THE IMPORTANCE OF UNDERSTANDING HALLUCINOGENS

Many questions arise when unraveling the complex, often contradictory nature of hallucinogens: Are hallucinogens as bad as other drugs? Do they cause long-term effects? Why do some groups continue to argue for the decriminalization of these substances?

Like these questions, hallucinogens themselves are complex. Generally speaking, serious health problems seem to be linked to the long-term use of these psychedelic substances. For sure, serious negative consequences in the form of irrational actions while under the influence of these drugs, even leading to death, occur frequently. Still, there remains much to be discovered about the exact scientific avenues through which hallucinogens impart their dream-like mental alterations.

Young adults in particular are part of the precise demographic most associated with the use of these drugs. Information is power, and understanding this mind-altering class of drugs leads one to see them for what they really are.

2

The History of Hallucinogens

On June 29, 1955, Gordon Wasson, a Vice President of J.P. Morgan &
Co, along with Allan Richardson, photographer, found themselves deep
in rural Mexico, about to be the first Westerners to document and take
part in an ancient mushroom ceremony.

Wasson and his wife had been studying mushrooms for the previous
30 years, and began a series of trips to partake in mushroom rituals.
The story of their quest and subsequent experiences with hallucinogenic
mushrooms was published in Life *magazine on May 13, 1957, receiving*
much attention and interest.

In the story, Wasson recounts his experiences while under the
influence of the drug. "We chewed and swallowed these acrid mush-
rooms," he said, "saw visions, and emerged from the experience awe-
struck." Describing the drug's effects, Wasson reported that, "It seemed
as though I was viewing a world of which I was not a part and with
which I could not hope to establish contact." Wasson goes on to say, "I
was seeing visions, for the effect of the mushrooms is to bring about a
fission of the spirit, a split in the person, a kind of schizophrenia, with
the rational side continuing to reason and observe the sensations that
the other side is enjoying."

In addition to his direct observations, Wasson found that the mush-
rooms did not seem to cause addiction and that an increase in dose
increased the strength of the hallucinations while not prolonging the
effect for any significant amount of time. After many trips Wasson and
his colleagues were able to identify seven different kinds of hallucinogenic

19

mushrooms. They called for further exploration and hoped to discover the chemical property within the mushrooms, which was subsequently discovered in 1958, by Albert Hofmann. Recognizing the vast history of hallucinogenic mushrooms among many cultures around the world, Wasson interestingly posited that perhaps it was under the influence of these mushrooms that man first entertained the idea of God or a higher power.

Natural hallucinogens have been used for thousands of years, in many societies, all over the world. Peyote and certain kinds of mushrooms containing hallucinogenic chemicals are the primary substances in this category. Evidence of their use, primarily for religious ceremonies or as medicines, appears among many archeological sites worldwide. This archeological evidence dates back as far as 9,000 years, while the first written records of hallucinogenic drug use occurred some 3,000 years ago. For example, one expedition uncovered a collection of hallucinogenic mushrooms in Texas, which was carbon dated to 5,000 B.C.[1]

WHAT ARE PSILOCYBIN MUSHROOMS?

Certain "magic" mushrooms can cause significant physical, visual, and perceptual changes when ingested. The primary effects of mushrooms come from several active **alkaloids** that they contain; the most common are psilocybin, psilocin, and baeocystin.

How are mushrooms used?
All psychoactive mushrooms are ingested. Recreational doses range from 1 to 5 grams, depending on the species and individual strength of the specimens (dosages for wet mushrooms are approximately 10 times higher).

What are the effects of mushrooms?
The primary effects of magic mushrooms last for four to six hours, though many users continue to experience some milder effects (e.g., trouble sleeping and a noticeable difference from reality) for an

(continues)

(continued)

additional two to six hours. As the effects of mushrooms intensify, a wide variety of perceptual changes may occur: pupil dilation, visuals, mental stimulation, new perspectives, feelings of insight, labile emotions, possible paranoia, and confusion. Closed-eye visuals are extremely common with psilocybin mushrooms. Open-eye visuals are common for some people and more likely at higher doses.

What are the side effects of "magic" mushrooms?

Many people experience nausea and/or vomiting after ingesting mushrooms, especially at higher doses. Anxiety and unwanted or frightening thoughts and visions are also possible. Mushrooms can cause strong, temporary changes in an individual's experience of life and reality. This mushroom trip can be a powerful psychoactive experience, especially at higher doses, and is significantly affected by experiences and setting. Mushrooms are neither physically addicting nor likely to cause psychological dependence.

What are some common street names for mushrooms?

Mushrooms are sometimes referred to as shrooms, cubes, or "magic" mushrooms.

Source: Institute for Substance Abuse Treatment Evaluation, "Hallucinogen," http://www.isate.memphis.edu/hallucinogen.html.

Researchers agree on the important role that psychoactive substances played in the lives of many early societies, yet the precise discovery of these plants remains unknown. Much research has occurred regarding the early use of hallucinogens (often in this context referred to as *entheogens*, literally meaning "God inside us"), among Native Americans groups in the United States. Peyote, which grows in Mexico and the southwestern United States, continues to be used in special ceremonies among these groups.

While these ceremonies differ from each other, they do follow a typical pattern. Generally a shaman (religious leader), along with those who are to participate in the ceremony, seek out and collect the peyote buds to be used. Given the relatively long effects (8–10 hours) of the drug, the participants

Figure 2.1 Native American Church peyote ceremony, Pine Ridge Indian Reservation, South Dakota. *(© shutterstock)*

gather at dusk and consume the buds, sometimes in the form of tea or alternatively as a powder. The drug begins to take effect within an hour. Songs are sung and prayers said, as the participants are swept up in the intense effects of mescaline. The ceremony typically continues through the night, ending at dawn, or when the effects of the drug wear off.

PSILOCYBIN MUSHROOMS

Like peyote, psilocybin mushrooms have been used by humans since the beginning of recorded history. Cave paintings and ancient artifacts, which depict the use of mushrooms, were found in Northern Algeria that date as far back as 5,000 B.C. In Central and South America, entire temples were built to honor the spirits of these "divine mushrooms." For example, in Central Mexico, the Mixtec culture worshipped the god Piltzintecuhtli, who was the god of hallucinatory plants, specifically the divine mushroom. Similarly, the Aztec culture worshipped a god called Xochipilli, who was the god of the "flowery dream," a term they used to refer to the psychedelic mushroom.[2]

WHAT IS PEYOTE?

Peyote is the common name for a small, turnip-shaped cactus native to Mexico. The active hallucinogenic material in peyote is mescaline.

How is peyote used?
The dried tops (commonly called buttons) of the cactus are eaten, brewed into a tea, or powdered and packaged into capsules. A hallucinogenic dose (about 5 grams of dried peyote) contains about 0.3 to 0.5 grams of mescaline, and the effects last about 12 hours.

How does peyote work?
Peyote alters perceptions, producing vivid hallucinations, inaccurate estimations of time, and feelings of anxiety.

What are the negative side effects of peyote use?
Peyote is not known to be physically habit-forming, but the desirable hallucinogenic effects of mescaline may cause users to seek out the drug. Impure or large doses of peyote can have toxic effects, such as nausea and depressed breathing.

Source: Institute for Substance Abuse Treatment Evaluation, "Hallucinogen," http://www.isate.memphis.edu/hallucinogen.html.

Following the Spanish conquest of the Aztecs in the 16th century, Catholic missionaries began to convert indigenous people to Christianity. As part of this process, the missionaries worked to suppress indigenous traditions, which included the use of psilocybin mushrooms. Commenting on the Aztec use of mushrooms, Spanish priest Bernardino de Sahagún, in the 17th century, wrote the following in his *Florentine Codex:* "The first thing to be eaten at the feast were small black mushrooms that they called nanacatl and bring on drunkenness, hallucinations and even lechery; they ate these before the dawn . . . with honey; and when they began to feel the effects, they began to dance, some sang and others wept. . . . When the drunkenness of the mushrooms had passed, they spoke with one another of the visions they had seen."

While the use of mushrooms had effectively been suppressed during the last several hundred years, their use never fully fizzled out; instead, the use of hallucinogenic mushrooms, as continued today, existed mostly as an underground phenomenon. The first written documentation of hallucinogenic mushrooms within Western medicinal literature came in 1799, in the *London Medical and Physical Journal*. Beyond this, interest in the study of mushrooms appreciably increased in the early 20th century, but little was learned until the 1950s, when R. Gordon Wasson and Valentina Pavlovna began to study the traditional use of mushrooms in Mexico. In 1955, Wasson and Pavlovna became the first Westerners to actively participate in an indigenous mushroom ceremony, which led to the publication of an article in *Life* magazine describing the experience. At the same time, Albert Hofmann, a research chemist at Sandoz Pharmaceuticals (a Swiss company), isolated psilocybin from the mushroom and developed a synthetic process for creating the molecule.

Inspired by the article in *Life* magazine, Timothy Leary, who was the director of psychiatric research at the Kaiser Family Foundation at the time, became interested in the subject, eventually also traveling to Mexico to experiment with hallucinogenic mushrooms firsthand. Upon his return, with the help of his associate Richard Alpert, Leary set up the Harvard Psilocybin Project at Harvard University, promoting the study of psilocybin and other hallucinogenic drugs. In subsequent years, after Harvard cancelled the project, Leary became a cult figure and advocate for the use of hallucinogens.

THE HISTORY OF LSD

During the first half of the 20th century, a great number of pharmaceutical companies were founded, resulting in a wide range of new medical discoveries. Working for Sandoz Pharmaceuticals (now Novartis), in Switzerland, Dr. Albert Hofmann began to experiment with **ergot**, a mold found on grains such as rye and wheat.[3] On November 16, 1938, hoping to create a compound that would stimulate breathing in asthma patients, Hofmann isolated the alkaloids within ergot, including **lysergic acid.** Hofmann prepared a derivative of lysergic acid, which he called LSD-25 since it was the 25th compound in the series. He then combined the lysergic acid with diethylamide, a synthetic compound, for further testing. Naming the compound LSD-25, the new compound was first tested on mice. While the scientist did notice erratic movements and strange twitching, no positive effects regarding respiratory function were noted. As a result, research on the compound was stopped, at least temporarily.

Figure 2.2 Albert Hofmann, inventor of LSD. *(Drug Enforcement Administration)*

Several years later, in 1943, Hofmann, who continued to believe that the drug had some positive effect, resumed testing. This time Hofmann set out to examine the stimulating properties of the drug, as he had noted in the

WHAT IS LSD?

LSD, the most potent mood and perception-altering drug known, is a clear or white, odorless, water-soluble material synthesized from lysergic acid, a compound derived from rye fungus. Oral doses as small as 30 micrograms can produce effects that last 6 to 12 hours.

How is LSD used?
LSD is initially produced in crystalline form. The pure crystal can be crushed to powder and mixed with binding agents to produce tablets known as "microdots" or thin squares of gelatin called "window panes." More commonly it is dissolved, diluted, and applied to paper or other materials. The most common form of LSD is "blotter acid," sheets of paper soaked in LSD and perforated into 1/4-inch square, individual dosage units.

How does LSD work?
LSD's effects typically begin 30 to 90 minutes after ingestion and may last as long as 12 hours. Colors, smells, sounds, and other sensations become highly intensified. Hallucinations distort or transform shapes and movements, and they may give rise to a perception that time is moving very slowly or that the user's body is changing shape. On some LSD "trips," users experience sensations that are enjoyable and mentally stimulating and that produce a sense of heightened understanding. Bad trips, however, may include terrifying thoughts and nightmarish

mice years earlier; it was at this point that an accidental and quite profound discovery occurred.

While transferring some of the compound from one glass beaker to another, Hofmann accidentally spilled a trace amount on one of his fingers. Within a short time the doctor started to feel the effect of the LSD chemical, an experience he later described in a letter to a colleague:

Last Friday, April 16, 1943, I was forced to interrupt my work in the laboratories in the middle of the afternoon and proceed home, being affected by a remarkable restlessness, combined with a slight dizziness.

feelings of anxiety and despair that include fear of insanity, death, or losing control. After five or six hours, users usually experience a "comedown," when sensations begin to subside. After about eight hours the trip is usually over, although residual effects may continue for several days.

What are LSD's side effects?
Users of LSD may experience some physiological effects, such as increased blood pressure and heart rate, dizziness, loss of appetite, dry mouth, sweating, nausea, numbness, and tremors. LSD can trigger underlying mental problems and produce **delusions**, paranoia, and **schizophrenia**-like symptoms. Persistent psychosis and hallucinogen persisting perception disorder (HPPD) may also occur. Many LSD users experience flashbacks, recurrences of certain aspects of a life experience (including a previous drug trip), long after ingestion of the drug. A flashback may occur suddenly, often without warning, and may occur within a few days or more than a year after LSD use. LSD users quickly develop a high degree of tolerance for the drug's effects. It is not considered an addictive drug, however, because it does not seem to produce compulsive drug-seeking behavior.

What are some of the street names for LSD?
Street names may include acid, blotter, boomers, or cubes.

Source: Institute for Substance Abuse Treatment Evaluation, "Hallucinogen," http://www.isate.memphis.edu/hallucinogen.html.

At home I lay down and sank into a not unpleasant intoxicated-like condition, characterized by an extremely stimulated imagination. In a dreamlike state, with eyes closed (I found the daylight to be unpleasantly glaring), I perceived an uninterrupted stream of fantastic pictures, extraordinary shapes with intense, kaleidoscopic play of colors. After some two hours this condition faded away.[4]

A few days later, suspecting that it had been the LSD that had caused the "dreamlike" effects, Hofmann decided to conduct a self-experiment, ingesting 250 micrograms of the substance. After about an hour, Hofmann began to experience the drastic psychedelic effects that we associate with LSD today. Convinced that he had made a significant discovery, Hofmann continued his research, looking into the possible use of the drug as a psychiatric tool. He never imagined that anyone would take the drug purely for recreational purposes.

LSD AND PSYCHOTHERAPY

After its initial discovery in the 1940s, research into the possible medicinal benefits of LSD continued and greatly expanded in the 1950s. Recognizing the psychological effects of the drug, much research was centered on investigating the potential effects of the drug on mental disorders, namely schizophrenia. At the time, the only treatment options for schizophrenia were antipsychotic drugs (essentially powerful sedatives), frontal lobotomy, and shock therapy. None of these treatment options were particularly successful, and they caused severe side effects. Because LSD caused effects similar to those present in

LSD AND THE CIA

While scientists in the 1950s and 1960s conducted numerous studies to determine any potential medicinal qualities associated with LSD, an alternate group of researchers, namely those at the Central Intelligence Agency (CIA), were busy conducting a different kind of experiment. During this time the CIA initiated what it called its MK-ULTRA project. The project involved covertly giving LSD to hundreds of participants, without their knowledge, and studying the effects. The goal of the project was to investigate how LSD could be used as a tool in combat, as a mind-control drug. Unfortunately the experiment involved the use of severe psychological torture, and many of the participants committed suicide or ended up in psychiatric wards. In the end the CIA was never held to account for MK-ULTRA or related experimentations of a similar nature.

Source: "Project MKULTRA, the CIA's Program of Research in Behavioral Modification: Joint Hearing before the Select Committee on Intelligence," August 3, 1977, http://www.nytimes.com/packages/pdf/national/13inmate_ProjectMKULTRA.pdf.

patients with psychotic disorders, scientists hoped to determine the process by which LSD acted on the brain, thereby formulating drugs to limit or block the effect of the chemical on the brain. These efforts, however, proved futile, as no major discoveries regarding LSD and potential psychotherapeutic treatments were found. Nevertheless LSD did help researchers understand mental illness in at least one respect: the realization that a chemical could cause such serious mind-altering effects. This meant that conditions such as schizophrenia might *also* have a chemical root, and thus would be treatable through the use of medications.

Schizophrenia, depression, and other disorders were not the only ailments for which LSD was studied as a potential medicine. Scientists also studied the effect of LSD on alcoholics and cancer patients. LSD, it seems, became a potential treatment option for all those conditions for which no treatment option was available.

Beyond this, many psychiatrists and research students ingested the drug in order to personalize their understanding of mental disorders. Some believed that taking the drug, which created some effects similar to psychosis, would result in greater insights into mental illness as a whole. But in the end, with limited results, LSD testing within the scientific community began to fade. This decline occurred in tandem with government pressure to clamp down on the drug. At the same time, many governments were increasingly alarmed at the crossover of the drug, from scientific research in the lab, into the wider society. Indeed by the early 1960s, LSD use occurred far outside the controlled boundaries of the laboratory.

LSD ENTERS MAINSTREAM CULTURE

LSD made the jump from scientific study to nationwide countercultural movement in the early 1960s. Aiding this transition were Timothy Leary, psychologist at Harvard University, and one of his colleagues, Richard Alpert. Together the two men cofounded the Harvard Psychedelic Drug Research Program, with the goal of studying the psychedelic and mystical effects of LSD. After years of study, Leary and his growing cadre of followers came to the belief that every human being could experience spiritual nirvana through the use of LSD. At a certain point Leary's project veered away from the scientific arena and into the area of dogma. He began to preach about the mystical benefits

Figure 2.3 Timothy Leary, a psychology instructor at Harvard University, was fired from his post in 1963 as a result of his experimentation with LSD. He went on to advocate the use of LSD throughout the 1960s and '70s.

of the drug. As Leary's studies turned into parties, Harvard eventually had no choice but to fire him. But he continued to promote LSD as its use continued to grow across the country. Because it was a relatively easy drug to make, the supply of LSD continued to grow (it was legal until late 1966), while the price of an individual dose continued to drop.[5]

As the use of LSD and other hallucinogens continued to increase during the 1960s, a backlash against their use emerged in tandem. An article in *Newsweek,* in February 1967, demonstrates the curiosity and growing skepticism of the emerging counterculture:

> They smile and call themselves a new race. They want to change the United States from within—by means of a vague regimen of all-embracing love. They are nonviolent, mystical, bizarre. Psychedelic drugs are their instant passport to Nirvana, a euphoric disdain for anything "square" is their most common bond. Like the beatniks of the '50s, they are in the long tradition of Bohemia: seeking a vision of totally free life. They are, of course, the hippies. . . . There is, of course, a low as well as a high side to the hippie phenomenon. In the Haight-Ashbury district, seriously disturbed people and teen-age runaways make up a sizeable fringe of the Movement. Equally unsettling is the incipient anti-intellectualism of the hippies—to say nothing of the dangers of drug-taking. The hippie's euphoria is too often brought at the price of his intellectual and critical faculties.[6]

As the 1960s rolled into the 1970s, with greater government and police efforts to curb LSD use, the drug slowly faded while other drugs, namely cocaine, took its place. LSD and its hallucinogenic family of drugs, however, never disappeared completely.

3
Chemical Properties and Effects of Hallucinogens

Gary was having a bad trip. It was about two hours after he'd taken the drug, an innocent-looking tab of acid. But now he was sweating, a lot. He was nervous and even shaking a little. In addition to the seemingly unstoppable sweat on his palms and forehead, he began to feel increasingly claustrophobic, almost as if he were trapped in a small space. He'd taken LSD a few times, but never had it been this frightening. In fact, he was trying to think of a time when he was more afraid and the thought made the "trip" even worse.

After another hour passed, it could accurately be said that Gary felt terrified. For one thing, he felt as if the universe was collapsing in on itself and he would inevitably be crushed. He kept trying to remind himself that it was only the effect of the drug but that didn't seem to help; he wondered how long the nightmare would last. He suddenly felt an overwhelming sense of depression and started to think that these feelings would never end. As time stood still, Gary started to believe that he was going insane and that he might have permanently damaged his brain. His heart raced and he started to yell loudly. He began to consider suicide, a thought that he'd never had before.

Having heard the anguished screams, the next-door neighbors called 911. When the ambulance arrived the medics found Gary in a wild, uncontrollable panic. Not aware of what was wrong, they carefully strapped Gary to a gurney and took him to the emergency room.

32

What is the brain mechanism underlying the mind-bending effects of hallucinogens such as LSD, mescaline, and psilocybin? According to experts, hallucinogens activate specific brain receptors called 5-HT2A receptors (2ARs); these receptors, they say, are normally triggered by the neurotransmitter serotonin. Because hallucinogens, as a class of drugs, involves several different drugs, the psychedelic effects can vary greatly, depending on the dose and specific type of drug. Many drugs in this class are considered "**designer drugs**" (as opposed to naturally existing drugs), and while the risk factors and toxicology of many hallucinogens are well documented, there is quite a wide spectrum of effects.

HALLUCINOGENS AND THE NERVOUS SYSTEM

Although the nervous system is often discussed in terms of peripheral and central components, it should be regarded as a highly integrated whole in which the central nervous (brain and spinal cord) plays a critical information gathering and processing role. The **peripheral nervous system** is often divided into the autonomic and somatic components, innervating the heart, gut, vasculature, and other internal organs and skeletal muscle, respectively. The **somatic nervous system** is responsible for voluntary body movements via muscle nerves, while the **autonomic nervous system** is often referred to as the "involuntary" system since it executes constant control over systems where we execute little or no conscious control, like breathing. The autonomic nervous system is divided into the sympathetic and parasympathetic components which typically exert opposing effects. Thus, the **sympathetic system** is involved in the "fight or flight" reaction that prepares the organism for stressful reactions (increased blood pressure and heart rate, accommodation for increased vision), while the **parasympathetic system** establishes a more relaxed situation (rest after a meal, for example). The autonomic nervous system that innervates the gut is sometimes called the enteric system and is responsible for the independent control of the mechanical and secretory functions of the gastrointestinal tract. Drugs, like hallucinogens, that affect the **central nervous system** may also have a major action in the gut. Although the nervous system is often regarded as a command or efferent system—sending instructions to be executed—there is also a sensory or afferent component that receives information from innervated systems and that is vital to the overall integrated nervous response. Finally, despite the anatomical and functional differences between the various components of the nervous system, they share a fundamental similarity in their use of chemicals—**neurotransmitters**—to convey information.

The individual unit of the nervous system is the **neuron,** a specialized cell that both receives and transmits information. The nervous system contains over 100 billion neurons and is a major user of metabolic energy in the human body. It is also a region particularly susceptible to injury from toxic chemicals, lack of oxygen, and other insults. Neurons in different nervous regions may have different anatomical features and may use different chemical transmitters. Neurons communicate with one another and with their end organs by these chemical signals, which are released from the nerve terminal and interact with specific receptors on adjacent neurons or cells.

The chemical transmitters may be small molecules—notably **acetylcholine**, **norepinephrine**, **epinephrine**, serotonin, **dopamine**, or histamine. Acetylcholine and norepinephrine are the dominant neurotransmitters in the parasympathetic and sympathetic nervous systems, respectively, while dopamine and serotonin, the neurotransmitters most associated with hallucinogens, are employed primarily in the central nervous system. These neurotransmitters serve to convey information between neurons—across the

THE PINEAL GLAND AND LSD

The **pineal gland** is located at the center of the brain and is about the size of a grain of rice. For a long time the function of the gland was thought to be only a vestige of a formerly important part of the brain. In the 20th century, however, scientists discovered that the pineal gland held an unusually high reservoir of serotonin, as compared to other parts of the brain. Researchers theorized that LSD and other hallucinogens work by stimulating the pineal gland, which in turn releases large amounts of serotonin, a neurotransmitter involved in emotion and sensory perception.

Source: Serena Roney-Dougal, "Walking Between the Worlds: Links between Psi, Psychdelics [sic], Shamanism and Psychosis: An Overview of the Literature," http://www.psi-researchcentre.co.uk/article_1.html.

synaptic cleft, a junction where two neurons meet, or across the neuroeffector junction, where neuron and the innervated organ meet (e.g., smooth, cardiac, or skeletal muscle; secretory gland).

Each neuron has specific synthetic machinery that enables it to both synthesize and eliminate a specific neurotransmitter. For example, neurons of the sympathetic nervous system employ norepinephrine and epinephrine as their transmitters. Other neurons, particularly in the central nervous system, employ dopamine as their transmitter. While there is still debate regarding the exact process through which hallucinogens affect the brain, perceptions, and the nervous system, it is generally believed that they bind to nervous cell receptor sites, normally affixed to serotonin.

THE CLASSIFICATION OF HALLUCINOGENS

Generally, hallucinogens are classified according to their mechanism of action, chemical structure, or quality of action. While these classifications often correlate in some way, classification of hallucinogens is made difficult by the fact

Table 3.1 Common Classification System for Hallucinogens
Dissociatives (NMDA/Sigma receptor antagonists)
– DXM (dextromethorphan) – Ketamine, Special K – PCP, angel dust – Nitrous oxide
Serotonergics (5-HT receptor agonists)
– DMT – Bufotenine – AMT – 5-MeO-AMT – DPT – DIPT – Psilocybin – LSD, acid
Phenylethylamines (Natural alkaloid)
– Mescaline – MDMA

that they often overlap in terms of effect and mechanism of action. One thing that almost all hallucinogens share is that they contain nitrogen and are most generally classified as *alkaloids*. Below this, common classification categories include dissociatives, serotonergics (drugs affecting serotonin receptor sites), and phenylethylamines. Table 3.1 displays a common classification system for hallucinogens.[1]

THE CHEMICAL PROPERTIES OF LSD

As we have already learned, LSD was invented in 1938 by Albert Hofmann, a Swiss chemist working for pharmaceutical company Sandoz. Hofmann's discovery of LSD came out of his experiments with a compound called ergot, which is essentially a fungus that attacks wheat plants, most notably rye. Ergot acts like a parasite, growing and developing symbiotically on the grass. Hofmann believed that there were medicinal properties within this parasitic compound.

Interestingly, prior to Hofmann's and other chemists' hypotheses that ergot contained useful medicinal properties, it had historically been maligned as a dangerous poison. It was first mentioned in the Middle Ages, as the principal cause of mass poisonings, affecting thousands of people at a time. Ingesting the compound resulted in convulsive and gangrenous effects. Up until the 17th century ergot continued to exist as a major health problem of epidemic proportions. It wasn't until the 17th century, when scientists discovered that ergot-containing bread was the cause of the mass poisonings, that its nasty effects were diminished. Improved farming techniques helped rid rye of the fungus. The last known epidemic associated with the fungus occurred from 1926–1927 in Russia.[2]

Beginning in the 1930s, a new era of ergot research began when scientists at the Rockefeller Institute of New York isolated the primary nucleus common to all ergot alkaloids. It was this nucleus which Hofmann studied in the late 1930s; they called it lysergic acid.

Working with the isolated lysergic acid, Hofmann's 25th combination of the basic chemicals showed some promise of medical benefits. As such, Sandoz introduced the drug, termed LSD-25 by Hofmann, under the trade name Delysid. It was marketed as a drug with psychiatric uses, but ultimately abandoned. LSD, as we know it today, is synthesized by reacting an activated form of lysergic acid with diethylamine, a flammable, strongly alkaline liquid. In its purest form, LSD is a bitter solid, both colorless and odorless. By the

Figure 3.1 Ergot (dark brown), a wheat fungus from which lysergic acid, the main ingredient of LSD, is derived. *(© Alamy)*

time LSD gets to an end user, it has typically been melted into a sugar cube or blotter paper for oral delivery. Because it only takes a very small amount of material to cause its effects, an extraordinary amount of LSD can be made by a small number of producers. According to the DEA, 25 kilograms of ergotamine tartrate can produce 5–6 kilograms of pure LSD crystal, which can in turn be processed into 100 million dosage units, the entire estimated annual U.S. demand for the hallucinogen.[3]

When a person consumes LSD, the drug binds to most serotonin receptor sites, acting as an agonist that is believed to increase the release of glutamate within the cerebral cortex. An agonist is a chemical that binds to a nervous cell's receptor site, triggering a response. In this case, as in the case of most hallucinogens, the chemical binds to receptor sites normally bound to serotonin, causing their psychedelic affects.

THE CHEMICAL PROPERTIES OF PSILOCYBIN MUSHROOMS

While there are many different species of psychedelic mushrooms, their common attribute is the psilocybin compound, a chemical with a structure very similar to serotonin. The chemical is produced by hundreds of species, including *Psilocybe semilanceata, Psilocybe cubensis,* and *Psilocybe cyanescens.* Once ingested, the body quickly **metabolizes** psilocybin, turning it into psilocin, which then acts as an agonist (a chemical that binds to a cell receptor site) at serotonin receptor sites in the brain.

THE CHEMICAL PROPERTIES OF MESCALINE

As we have learned, mescaline is a chemical produced naturally in certain plants, specifically cacti. More specifically, it is found in the peyote cactus, San Pedro cactus, the Peruvian Torch cactus, and also certain members of the bean family. Because the taste of the cacti is usually very bitter, users typically grind the plant into a powder, integrate it into tea, or re-form it into capsules.

While each cactus button contains about 25 milligrams of mescaline, the average human dose ranges anywhere from 178 to 356 mg of mescaline hydrochloride, thus several buttons are required for a single dose. Once ingested, most of the mescaline is metabolized by the body, but up to half of the amount ingested is excreted in the urine unchanged. The remaining metabolized quantity affects the peripheral nervous system. Specifically, like other hallucinogens, mescaline activates the serotonin receptor, acting as an agonist at the 5-HT2A receptor site. Also like other hallucinogens, the exact mechanism by which mescaline acts remains unknown.

THE PHYSIOLOGICAL AND PSYCHOLOGICAL EFFECTS OF HALLUCINOGENS

The physical effects of hallucinogens most often involve enhanced or altered perceptions. The altered perceptions relate to all five of the senses. Sounds are subverted, visual hallucinations may occur, a subtle breeze may cause increased sensations on the skin, and taste and smell are greatly augmented. These effects are most likely the result of the buildup of serotonin in the brain and may last for as long as 12 hours, depending upon the specific hallucinogen and dosage. Users report drastic changes in mood, swinging between comic hysteria and deep sadness.

The sense of hunger may increase or decrease and the ability to control muscles may be altered. The body reacts in other ways, too; body temperature increases, often causing profuse sweating, and one's heart rate speeds up as well. Under the influence of hallucinogens, sleeping becomes difficult. One of the better fictional accounts of the effects of hallucinogens is found in the anonymously written classic book *Go Ask Alice:*

> Suddenly I began to feel something strange inside myself like a storm. I remember that two or three records had played since we had had the drinks, and now everyone was beginning to look at me. The palms of my hands were sweating and I could feel droplets of moisture on my scalp at the back of my neck. My whole body was tense at every muscle and a feeling of weird apprehension swept over me, strangled me, suffocated me.[4]

While these are some of the general effects of hallucinogens, each drug causes slightly different reactions. Moreover, hallucinogens are highly specific in terms of the user. That means that different people react differently, even when taking the exact same drug. The difference depends on natural levels of serotonin, as not everyone maintains similar levels. For example, a person with a higher natural level of serotonin will have a more severe and intense experience.[5] Many people experience what is known as a "bad trip." In this case the user's altered perceptions become intensely frightening and horrific. Most often the sensation is compared to a nightmare that will not end. The user's state of mind greatly affects how he will experience the drug.

In addition to the effects already discussed, LSD has been known to cause numbness, weakness, nausea, **hypothermia** or **hyperthermia**, elevated blood sugar, jaw clenching, even tremors. Under the influence of psilocybin, users report lethargy and drastic shifts between feelings of **euphoria** and depression. Another effect of the drug is called "closed eye hallucination." As the name suggests, this means that even with eyes closed, the user sees multi-colored geometric shapes and other startling visual images. Mescaline, in particular, enhances visual imagery, which is often described as a kaleido-scopic sensation. PCP is quite different than the other hallucinogens. While PCP does cause perceptual distortions, it is also a dissociative, which causes feelings of detachment and leaves the user feeling impervious to pain, much like an anesthetic. Users of PCP report severe anxiety, symptoms that mimic schizophrenia, delusions, and paranoia; long-term users report memory loss as well. Another notable difference is that PCP, unlike other hallucinogens, is addictive. Most hallucinogens cause what is termed as "rapid tolerance build up," which means the body reaches a point where it will simply excrete, rather than metabolize, any more of the drug. For this reason, users gain no added effect by taking additional dosages.

The long-term effects of hallucinogens are mostly relegated to the area of psychology. While more study is needed, researchers believe that long-term use of hallucinogens changes the brain in significant ways.[6] Though still debated, one school of thought contends that psychedelics, such as MDMA, release neurotransmitters that cause increased formation of free radicals. In turn, it is believed that these free radicals are associated with the onset of **Parkinson's disease**, senility, schizophrenia, and Alzheimer's.[7] Finally, the most commonly experienced mid- to long-term side effect of hallucinogen use is known as hallucinogen persisting perception disorder (HPPD), commonly referred to as a flashback. This is a condition where the effect of the drug returns suddenly, a week, month, or even a year later.

Clearly, the use of hallucinogens causes euphoria as well as a range of seri-ous negative effects. Perhaps the most perilous effect of all is the unknown—as the user typically has no idea what is actually in the drug or what effect it will have. Even so, the use and abuse of hallucinogens continues.

4

The Use and Abuse of Hallucinogens

The chemist, having obtained the lysergic acid derivative from ergot, dissolves the substance in a methanoic KOH solution before removing the methanol by using a vacuum system. With the remaining residue, more KOH solution is added and heated for an hour. While it heats, the chemist allows a stream of nitrogen gas to pass through the flask. The alkaline solution that's left after this process is filtered and purified; the lights in the laboratory are brought down, like a dark room, to ensure that the volatile compound doesn't decompose. The chemist makes sure to wear rubber gloves because the ergot alkaloids he's using are highly poisonous. Before he's finished, the chemist will perform many more manipulations, additions, and dissolutions to the chemical he's making. After several days of work, the chemist will have made a batch of LSD, ready to send out across the United States, to people who will have no idea where the drug came from, or who was responsible for its production.

Hallucinogen **dependence** is generally defined as the continued use of hallucinogens, even when the substances cause the affected individual significant problems, or when the user knows of the adverse effects (memory impairment while intoxicated, anxiety attacks, flashbacks), but continues to use the substances anyway. "Craving" hallucinogens after not using them for a period of time has been reported. Hallucinogen **abuse** is the repeated use of hallucinogens, even after they have caused the user impairment that undermines his ability to fulfill obligations at work, school, or home.

41

Hallucinogens distort and intensify auditory and visual sensations. For example, users may feel as if they are seeing sounds and hearing colors. People feel as if they are not real (called depersonalization) or are detached from their environment (called dissociation). Many hallucinogens cause nausea and vomiting. LSD causes blurred vision, sweating, palpitations, and impaired coordination. The actual effect can depend on the user's mood, expectations when the drug is taken, and the setting in which the drug is consumed. That said, this chapter will focus on the use of hallucinogens, how users obtain the drugs, their long-term effects, signs of **addiction**, and how their use affects the user's life as well as those around him.

THE HISTORY OF HALLUCINOGEN ABUSE

Many hallucinogens did not come into popular use until relatively recently. While certain hallucinogens, like mescaline and psilocybin mushrooms, have indeed been used for thousands of years, their overall use remains comparatively small. But with the advent of LSD in the 1960s, two groups emerged to support hallucinogen use. The first was in the academic setting, led by people like writer Aldous Huxley, who felt that LSD was too powerful to be released to the masses, but that it could be used among elite members of society— writers, artists, scientists, and the like. Contrarily, a second group emerged, led by infamous LSD proponents like Timothy Leary, who believed that hallucinogens like LSD could transform society for the better. They advocated widespread use of these substances.

As a result of these early attempts to celebrate hallucinogen use, claiming that they could provide religious experiences and enhanced artistic activity, their use gained a strong foothold in society. According to the National Household Survey on Drug Abuse, by 1972, 5% of Americans (almost all under the age of 18) had used psychedelics at least once. As that cohort of users grew older, the overall figure increased; in 1979, the peak of LSD use in America, 25% of young adults aged 18–25 reported use of hallucinogens. This rise occurred despite a conclusion published by the National Institute of Mental Health in 1974, which found that LSD had no therapeutic use.[1] In that same year, 17% of all Americans reported use of hallucinogens.

In the early 1980s, the use of hallucinogens began to decline. In 1982, while 6% of adults over 26 years old reported lifetime use of hallucinogens, less than 1% reported use in the prior year. It seems, as the initial cohort of hallucinogen users got older, they ceased using these substances. At the same time new waves of young adults did not use hallucinogens in the same numbers as before. Experts believe that there are two explanations for this downward trend in the 1980s. First, it seems that a general understanding permeated society that hallucinogens provide no therapeutic benefit, instead resulting in a host of unwanted long-term side effects. Second, it is generally recognized that LSD and other hallucinogens simply fell out of fashion, as cocaine became the drug de rigueur in America at the time.

This trend changed in the 1990s. As early as 1992, researchers began to notice an uptick in the availability of hallucinogens throughout many parts of the country. Experts agreed that this was a direct result of the emerging "rave" music scene, in which hallucinogens played a prime role. Researchers also found that this subset of drug was particularly used within a certain sector of the population, namely affluent white males and females. By the early 2000s, the uptick in hallucinogen use could be seen within national statistics, showing that the overall use, while not on par with the level of the use in the 1960s, was on the rise again.

Studies focused on pinpointing where in the United States hallucinogens are used found that urban and suburban areas, as well as college campuses, saw greater use of hallucinogens. Use of these substances was not limited to one area of the country, however, as it was found to be relatively consistent across the nation. Toward the end of the 1990s, newer synthetic hallucinogens, such as MDMA and ketamine, gained in popularity relative to traditional hallucinogens like LSD and psilocybin. Though not exclusively, in the main these drugs were used as **club drugs**.

Studies of college campuses show that while alcohol and marijuana are by far the most typical drugs used, hallucinogen use is also common. In one study, 44% of colleges reported widespread use of hallucinogens on their campuses.[2] Public and private universities show similar patterns of use, while religious schools are least likely to report widespread hallucinogen use. Further, those colleges in or close to urban areas are more likely to report higher numbers of this type of drug use.

Well into the first decade of the 21st century, hallucinogen use in the United States is widely prevalent once again. According the National Survey on Drug Use and Health, in 2006, approximately 23 million people aged 12 or older had used LSD in their lifetime, or 9.5% of the population. Of that very large figure, however, less than 700,000 had used LSD within the past year.[3] Overall, persons aged 18 to 25 were more likely to be past-year users than those older than 25 or younger than 18. Generally speaking, men are more likely to be users than females; however, females aged 12 to 17 are more likely than males in this group to have used Ecstasy, a synthetic drug similar to LSD, in the past year. According to the report, 2.3 million people aged 12 or older reported use of ketamine within their lifetime (203,000 were past-year users) and almost 700,000 people had used dimethyltryptamine (DMT), alpha-methyltryptamine (AMT), or 5-methoxy-diisopropyltryptamine (Foxy) (100,000 within the past year). Finally, approximately 1.8 million people aged 12 or older had used *Salvia divinorum,* a naturally occurring hallucinogenic herb, in their lifetime. Another study, conducted by the National Institute on

FACT OR MYTH? ABSINTHE IS A HALLUCINOGEN

For many, absinthe is a well-known and highly controversial alcoholic drink, with hallucinogenic properties. Although typically labeled a liqueur, absinthe is rightly classified as a spirit (i.e., there is no added sugar in the drink). Nevertheless the spirit is indeed copiously alcoholic at levels between 45% and 74% alcohol. The anise-flavored drink originated in Switzerland and became very popular in the 19th and early-20th century, in part with the help of a few famous fans of the beverage. These were bohemian artists such as Vincent van Gogh and Oscar Wilde.

Due to its portrayal as not just another alcoholic drink, but rather a dangerous psychoactive drug, absinthe was banned in the United States and throughout Europe by 1915, though today it is available once again. A chemical called **thujone**, present in small quantities in the spirit, was blamed for its hallucinogenic properties.

Today it is known that thujone does not cause hallucinations and absinthe is clearly not a hallucinogen. Yet the belief that this highly alcoholic beverage has unique mind-altering properties continues to be embraced by many.

Drug Abuse, found that there were no significant changes in hallucinogen use in 2007 and 2008. It was noted, however, that the perceived harm caused by hallucinogens decreased among 12th-graders, from 67.3% in 2007, to 63.6% in 2008. This signals a significant attitude shift, which could result in elevated use of these substances overall.[4]

PRODUCTION AND DISTRIBUTION OF HALLUCINOGENS

The production of LSD has been illegal since the 1960s, yet a small number of producers, believed to be operating in Northern California, manufacture most of the nation's LSD. In fact it is estimated that less than a dozen chemists, who have likely operated since the 1960s, supply all of the LSD for the United States. Thus LSD manufacturers can basically be divided into two groups, with this small group as the first. The second are small, independent producers who distribute only on a local level and as a result are less of a concern to drug enforcement agents.

It takes specific knowledge of organic chemistry to produce LSD. Careful laboratory procedures and specific scientific tools must be acquired. This, in part, helps explain why there are so few producers. These chemists, often referred to as "cooks," are said to exist almost as a fraternity, a very close-knit group. While most are believed to be trained scientists, those that are not must have been personally trained by a chemist. The high level of education, combined with their small number, help producers to evade law enforcement officials.

Another advantage that producers have is the small amount of product needed to make a huge number of doses. Unlike marijuana or cocaine, large quantities of raw material are not required to produce the drug. For example, only 25 kilograms of ergotamine tartrate result in 5–6 kilograms of pure LSD crystal, enough to produce 100 million doses, or the entire U.S. demand for the hallucinogen.

One difficulty that LSD cooks have is acquiring the raw material, ergotamine tartrate. This is the starting point for LSD manufacture and the material cannot be found in the United States. Ergotamine tartrate is a highly regulated substance; thus manufacturers are forced to seek it from other places around the world namely in Europe, Mexico, Costa Rica, and Africa.

Once the raw material is acquired, it takes two to three days to produce 1 to 4 ounces of pure LSD crystal. Producers generally make small batches to ensure that as little of the raw material is lost as possible, and it ensures that if a batch becomes contaminated, it does not waste all of the product.

Once in pure crystal form, LSD is diluted and usually absorbed into blotter paper for distribution. Generally speaking, 1 gram of crystal could produce 20,000 dosages of LSD; however, producers often dilute it even further to increase profits. Studies of LSD samples over the years indicate that the average dose is about 62% pure in its final form.

Once manufactured, LSD follows the typical pattern of drug distribution. From the few small producers at the top of the chain, product is distributed to major urban centers first, followed by more widespread distribution. This process happens relatively quickly as LSD is highly susceptible to heat, air, and time degradation. In other words, if not distributed quickly, the doses will lose their potency; they do not have a long shelf life.

Distribution of other synthetic hallucinogens happens in much the same way, but on an even smaller scale. Natural hallucinogens, like psilocybin mushrooms, which also exist on a relatively small scale, are foraged from the ground, transported, and dispersed by a loose network of traffickers. Because mushrooms, like LSD, are relatively easy to disguise, law enforcement agencies have great difficulty stemming the distribution of hallucinogens.

HALLUCINOGEN ADDICTION AND LONG-TERM EFFECTS

Hallucinogens are unique among other classes of illicit drugs in that, for the most part, they are not considered to be addictive. The effects of these drugs are so intense and last for so long that they literally exhaust the body. This is in great contrast to other substances, like cocaine, which exert very intense but rapid effects that quickly subside. As a result, the cocaine user, for example, will likely continue to abuse the drug over and over again in a single night. Researchers have found that hallucinogen users do not continually abuse these drugs in rapid succession, but instead use these drugs occasionally rather than habitually. Still, over time, hallucinogens can exert long-term health effects. The intense nature of these drugs means that even a small number of uses may result in long-term psychological effects. Currently, however, these long-term effects are not well understood.

EFFECT ON FAMILY AND FRIENDS

As with most drugs, the effect of LSD goes beyond its influence, both physical and psychological, on the user alone. The effect of hallucinogens on the long-term user will no doubt affect relationships with family and friends in unknown ways. It is very likely, too, that the hallucinogen user will abuse other drugs, which in some cases may lead to severe debilitation. The user may lose his job, fail out of school, or end up in jail, causing great anguish for family members. Parents especially may feel helpless and that they've somehow failed. For sure, the effects will vary depending on the individual, nature of the abuse, and ability to overcome it. While there are many unknowns, one thing is certain: The use of hallucinogens will not improve familial relations, take away problems, or result in more friends.

5
Treatment and Recovery

A young woman is brought to the emergency room by a group of friends. The woman's mental state shifts wildly between what seems like euphoria and extreme agitation. In response to questions concerning her name, address, and what time it is, the patient demonstrates general alertness but a very loose thought process. Upon further questioning, the patient's friends say that they had been at a party where alcohol was consumed, but do not disclose the presence of any illegal substances. Physical symptoms include an increased body temperature, a flushed appearance, decreased perspiration, and increased heart rate. When asked directly, the patient indicates the she consumed a "magic tea." It is determined that the patient is under a hallucinogenic substance, most likely LSD. Increasingly agitated, the patient is treated with Valium and removed to a quiet hospital room for further monitoring.

Acute treatment for the use of hallucinogens is aimed at preventing the patient from harming himself or anyone else. Since most people experiencing hallucinogen intoxication remain in touch with reality, "talking down" is often helpful—offering reassurance and support that emphasizes that the "bad trip," anxiety, **panic attack**, or **paranoia** will pass as the drug wears off. Patients are kept in a calm, pleasant, but lighted environment, and are encouraged to move around while being helped to remain oriented to reality. Occasionally drugs such as **lorazepam** are given for anxiety. Complications in treatment occur when the hallucinogen has been contaminated with other street drugs or chemicals. Treatment options for long-term effects of hal-

48

lucinogen use involve long-term psychotherapy after drug use has stopped. Many people find 12-step programs or group support helpful. In addition, underlying psychiatric disorders must be addressed. In addition to the short-term and long-term treatment options for hallucinogen use, it is important to understand success statistics from treatment programs as well as how one goes about receiving treatment.

WHEN IS TREATMENT REQUIRED?

The effects of hallucinogens are primarily mental, as opposed to physical (though there are physical consequences). For the most part, use of hallucinogens will go untreated, unless the user experiences what is commonly known as a "bad trip."

For sure, not all hallucinogen-induced experiences result in mind-expanding epiphanies, entertaining hallucinations, or spiritual awakenings. Sometimes the user spirals into a panic-stricken state, perhaps best described as a very long nightmare. Researchers believe that a bad trip occurs for three main reasons. Perhaps the most commonly cited reason for a bad trip is an overdose; in the case of LSD, this would occur when a person consumes more than 250 micrograms. At that level, the brain is literally overwhelmed with the release of serotonin. The second factor is environment; if the user does not feel comfortable, or is in an unfamiliar setting without familiar faces, it may lead to a bad trip. Thirdly, the psychological state of the individual is believed to strongly impact whether or not the user will experience a bad trip.

Whether the result of an overdose, negative environment, or predisposed psychological state, a bad trip is what usually causes the user to seek medical attention for the first time. The first step in addressing a user experiencing a bad trip is to try to calm him down. Essentially, the treatment for a bad trip is analogous to treating a panic or anxiety attack. It is common for the user to feel as if the negative experience will never end, that they have somehow become trapped in a psychotic state over which they have no control. At this point the user will probably exhibit irrational thinking, which could lead to violent behavior. For example, users experiencing bad trips have been known to jump out of windows, dive into bodies of water, become uncontrollable, and even commit suicide. Thus initially, the main concern is to prevent the user from harming himself or others.

WHAT IS PMA?

PMA (Paramethoxyamphetamine) is an illicit, synthetic hallucinogen that has stimulant effects similar to Ecstasy (MDMA).

How is PMA used?
PMA is typically administered orally in pill or capsule form. PMA powder, although uncommon, may be inhaled or injected to accelerate the response.

What are PMA's side effects?
Side effects may include increased pulse rate and blood pressure, increased and labored respiration, elevated body temperature, erratic eye movements, muscle spasms, nausea, and heightened visual stimulation. Higher doses can produce cardiac arrhythmia, breathing problems, pulmonary congestion, renal failure, hypothermia, vomiting, convulsions, coma, and possibly death.[1]

To calm the user down, it is suggested that they be taken to a relaxed setting, with low light and few stimuli. The user should be informed and reminded that it is the drug that is causing the effect and that he is not actually going crazy. It is important, at this point, to affirm that the effect of the drug will wear off, contrary to what the user may believe. As the effect of the drug can last for many hours, this process may indeed be a long one. In some instances a user may be so far gone that they cannot be "talked down." In this situation the only remaining recourse is to go directly to the nearest hospital.

SHORT-TERM TREATMENT FOR HALLUCINOGEN USE

When someone arrives at the hospital emergency room, and is believed to be under the influence of a hallucinogen like LSD, the user is treated as if they have been poisoned. The first step is to assess and stabilize the patient's airway, breathing, and circulation. Next, the nurse or doctor will try to determine the exact substance the user has taken, how much, and whether or not

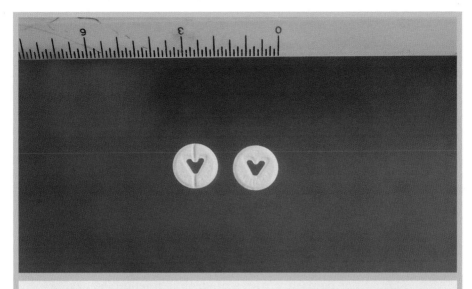

Figure 5.1 Valium, a tranquilizer, may be administered for emergency treatment of an individual who has taken LSD. *(Drug Enforcement Administration)*

it was mixed with other substances, such as alcohol. It is likely that the patient will be placed in a quiet setting and, if found to be highly volatile, may be temporarily restrained (though sometimes this only increases the patient's excitation).

If the patient is unable to be calmed down verbally, she will be treated with fast-acting **benzodiazepines** like diazepam, lorazepam, or triazolam. Essentially, these are antianxiety medications commonly used to treat panic and anxiety attacks. If the patient is still locked in a psychotic state, the next step is to treat with a more powerful sedative, such as thorazine. Importantly, none of these drugs will actually end the "bad trip"; rather they will temper the release of serotonin, with the aim to ease the patient's sense of panic.

TREATMENT PROGRAMS

While short-term treatment using antianxiety medications and sedatives will help realign the patient's mental condition, some situations will require follow-up with long-term psychological treatment and monitoring. Such treatment programs for hallucinogen use do exist but are generally combined programs.

MEDICATIONS USED FOR HALLUCINOGEN TREATMENT

The goal of providing medication to a patient under the influence of hallucinogens is to neutralize the effects of the toxic agent, calm the patient and attempt to restore mental stability, and to avoid complications. The typical drugs used are as follows: [2]

Benzodiazepines: Sedation and anxiolytic properties help to calm an agitated patient and reduce any coexisting hypertension and tachycardia.

- Lorazepam (Ativan)—Sedative hypnotic that increases action of GABA, a major inhibitory neurotransmitter in the brain. May depress all levels within the central nervous system. Should not be used if traces of alcohol, phenothiazines, or barbiturates are present.
- Diazepam (Valium)—Depresses all levels of central nervous system. Should not be used if traces of alcohol, phenothiazines, or barbiturates are present.

Neuroleptics: Used for patients demonstrating severe agitation and/or psychosis.

- Haloperidol (Haldol)—Haloperidol is in a group of medications called conventional antipsychotics. It works by decreasing abnormal excitement in the brain.

Antidotes: Used to treat secondary effects of hallucinogen use such as an abnormal blood-sugar level or thiamine deficiency, or to reverse opioid effects.

- Dextrose (D-glucose)—Regulates glucose level.
- Thiamine (Thiamilate)—Used to correct a thiamine deficiency.
- Nalaxone (Narcan)—While the exact mode of action is unknown, the medication seems to reverse opioid effects.

Treatment counselors find that people who use hallucinogens almost never do so without use of other drugs. Thus typically those who have used hallucinogens also require treatment for other illicit substances. Anecdotal reports from treatment counselors indicate that around 80% of patients in drug treatment programs have used hallucinogens at some point. In terms of specific treatment options, there is no magic-bullet medicinal solution, only programs that separate users from the drug and provide emotional support to patients. In the end the only true long-term treatment option for hallucinogen use is self-restraint.

NARCOTICS ANONYMOUS

The single largest treatment program for drug abusers, including those who abuse hallucinogens, is Narcotics Anonymous (NA). An offshoot of Alcoholics Anonymous (AA), NA is based on a 12-step program of recovery. NA considers itself a "fellowship or society of men and women for whom drugs had become a major problem."[3] Membership to NA does not require any payment of fees, nor religious, political, or any other orientation; membership requires one thing: the "desire to stop using."

Narcotics Anonymous has existed for many years, initially established in the late 1940s in California. The program was designed as a sister program to AA, to focus solely on addiction associated with drug use. Officially founded in 1953, NA started as a small group but is now one of the largest organizations of its kind. With fewer than 200 registered groups in 1978, today there are more than 25,000 NA groups holding almost 44,000 weekly meetings in 127 countries.

NA is designed not to address specific drug addictions per se, but rather to treat the source of the problem, which it generally referred to as addiction. As a result, NA does not refer to drugs, or drug abuse, in its literature at all. Rather, NA views addiction as a disease for which there is no known cure. It is a disease that affects every facet of the addict's life: mental, physical, emotional, and spiritual.

On a practical level NA works by creating a small support group, where each group holds regular fellowship meetings. These meetings take place wherever is convenient, be it libraries, community centers, churches, or hospitals. While meetings vary in format, they typically involve the reading of NA literature, followed by sharing of stories, either by a selected speaker or general sharing by group members. Each meeting ends with a nondenominational prayer. One of the most important parts of the NA recovery process is sponsorship. While certainly not mandatory in order to attend, members are encouraged to seek a sponsor, typically a more senior member of the NA group, who will serve as a guide through the 12 steps and provide support in times of need. An important part of NA is anonymity, which means that usually members will only refer to each other by first names.

Because NA does not maintain statistics of its membership, or track recovery rates for its members, it is hard to determine the program's level of success. Nevertheless, its long history and wide membership suggest that it works. In terms of demographics, again, specific data is not maintained. However, a survey of thousands of members at the 2003 NA World Convention found the following information:[4]

- *Gender:* 55% male, 45% female
- *Age:* 3% 20 years old and under, 12% 21–30 years old, 31% 31–40 years old, 40% 41–50 years old, 13% over the age of 51.
- *Ethnicity:* 70% Caucasian, 11% African American, 11% Hispanic, 8% other.
- *Employment Status:* 72% employed full time, 9% employed part time, 7% unemployed, 3% retired, 3% homemakers, 5% students, and 1% not answering.
- *Recovery:* Continuous recovery ranged from less than one year to more than 40 years with an average of 7.4 years.

To contact NA or find a local meeting, call the fellowship services staff at (818) 773–9999, extension #771.

6
Hallucinogens and the Law

In late 2000, the Drug Enforcement Administration pulled off one of the largest LSD busts in U.S. history; the target was Leonard Pickard. Born in California in 1945, Pickard would become one of the high priests of LSD manufacture. A trained chemist, Pickard attended Princeton and received a degree from Purdue University. More recently he worked as the deputy director of UCLA's Drug Policy Research Program. But while leading a distinguished life in public, Pickard also led a clandestine life as one of the largest producers of LSD in the nation. Pickard was first arrested in December 1988, in Mountain View, California. A neighbor had reported a strange smell emanating from a nearby warehouse. Upon inspection, DEA officials found a high-tech LSD lab hidden in a trailer within the warehouse. As a result, Pickard served five years in prison. After he was released, Pickard attended Harvard University but continued to produce LSD. He operated very secretively, moving his laboratory occasionally, from Oregon to Colorado to New Mexico. In 2000, however, in Wamego, Kansas, officials uncovered his lab and arrested Pickard once again. This time they discovered that the lab had been producing about a kilogram of material every five weeks, which they estimated would result in 10 million doses. As one of the largest LSD busts in history, this time Pickard was put away for good; he is now serving out two lifetime sentences in Tucson, Arizona.

The past 50 years have witnessed considerable debate among policy makers over the legal status of hallucinogens, but that debate has yet to reach a clear resolution. Five decades of illicit hallucinogen use by millions of Americans, coupled with legitimate scientific research, have prompted many people to challenge government claims that hallucinogens represent a serious health risk to individuals and to the nation in general. At the heart of this disagreement are the standards that, since 1970, have been used to classify certain drugs as illicit while others are listed as legal. As of 2010, most well-known hallucinogens are illegal in most Western countries. Hallucinogens are relatively inexpensive, domestically produced, and not part of a network of distributors battling over markets or territory. The legal repercussions in the United States for the possession for hallucinogens are on par with other illegal drugs.

PRODUCTION AND DISTRIBUTION

As previously discussed in this volume, a big difference between the production of hallucinogens, namely LSD, and other illegal substances is the vastly different amounts of product needed. For LSD, a small amount of active ingredient, ergotamine tartrate, translates into the number of doses required to meet the entire U.S. demand. Therefore, as we have learned, it is believed that just a handful of manufacturers concentrated in Northern California are responsible for the entire U.S. supply. During the 1980s, when drug enforcement officials confiscated a large number of doses from across the country, they were surprised to find that the doses were of consistently high purity, between 20 and 80 micrograms.[1] This further confirmed that most doses were originating from a few producers. The DEA compares the group of producers to a fraternity or a small club, with high levels of secrecy involved. As a result, while it is believed that at least some of these producers have been manufacturing LSD for 30, even 40 years, they have remained largely unchallenged by law enforcement.

The DEA notes that in addition to the major producers, there exists a larger web of local producers, who manufacture small amounts of product with lower potencies. Generally speaking, the DEA is less concerned with these local producers, focusing instead on the largest networks. And while California is viewed as the epicenter of LSD production in the United States, there is also production in other countries. Notably, after LSD was made illegal in the United States, it was discovered that approximately 35 million doses were imported from Europe via a man named Ronald Stark.[2] As the last country to produce LSD legally until 1975, Czechoslovakia produced much of the California acid at that time. In 1969, in the United Kingdom, Quentin Theobald and Peter Simmons were busted for LSD production in Kent and an apartment in London, respectively; it was the largest LSD bust in the United Kingdom up until that point. Similar busts continued in the United Kingdom and in Europe throughout the following decades. Perhaps the most famous bust was the one dubbed "Operation Julie." Headed by chemist Richard Kemp, the UK-based operation, thought to be the largest in the world at the time, was broken up in 1978. More recently DEA agents have discovered and seized large amounts of mimic LSD doses. These blotter papers were laced with other hallucinogenic chemicals, called DOB and DOC, in place of lysergic acid. In 2000, the large bust of acid manufacturer Leonard Pickard in Kansas resulted in a great decline of LSD availability throughout the United States.

THE HISTORY OF DRUG CONTROL

Unlike the history of hallucinogen use, the history of drug control is comparatively short. In the United States, drug control dates back to the 1840s, when the National Drug Import Law was passed by Congress to ensure that imported drugs were properly labeled. Before this, drugs were totally unregulated by the U.S. government and there were no established definitions for prescription and nonprescription drugs, narcotics, or drug abuse. Furthermore, there were no laws requiring manufacturers of drugs to report the quantity and distribution of drugs produced, conduct tests to make sure that drugs were safe, or carry out clinical trials to prove a drug's efficacy. In fact, until the 1906 Pure Food and Drug Act, anyone could make or take a concoction or sell any drug to anyone without fear or influence of any government agency. The world we live in today, however, is very different as drug policies, agencies, and laws have continually grown and evolved. Here are a few of the highlights:

- Pure Food and Drug Act (1906): Arguably the most important piece of food and drug legislation in American history, the 1906 act defined both *drug* and *misbranding* and was designed to eliminate false claims. The act led directly to the creation of the Food and Drug Administration (FDA).

- Shirley Amendment (1912): Soon after the 1906 act, it was realized that there were innumerable violations that needed attention. The Shirley Amendment was the first attempt by the government to remove fraudulent drugs (drugs that did not do what they claimed to do) from the market.
- Food, Drug, and Cosmetics Act (1938): This law required drug manufacturers to document and prove the safety of all their drugs and report their findings to the FDA.
- Durham-Humphrey Act (1951): This law made a distinction, for the first time, between prescription and nonprescription drugs. As a result, many medications could only be obtained through a physician's prescription.
- Kefauver-Harris Amendment (1962): This law dealt with the effectiveness of new drugs. Drug manufacturers now had to prove that their drugs were not only safe but effective as well.
- The FDA designates LSD an experimental drug and restricts research and the first LSD-related arrests are made (1962).
- LSD becomes illegal in California (1966).
- Controlled Substances Act (CSA) (1970): This important piece of legislation outlines the control, evaluation, and penalties of all narcotic agents and other dangerous drugs. The CSA defines a scheduling system for drugs. As part of this system, most of the known hallucinogens, including LSD, psilocybin, psilocin, mescaline, peyote, and MDMA, are placed in the schedule.

MODERN DRUG CONTROL

Throughout the years countless laws have been added or adjusted to deal with the changing drug culture in America, from focusing heavily on alcohol in the 1920s, to psychedelic drugs in the 1960s. In recent history the most important legislative action regarding drugs was the Controlled Substances Act (CSA) of 1970. Put into effect on May 1, 1971, the CSA was a sweeping law that replaced more than 50 previous drug bills. The primary implication

| Table 6.1 DEA Hallucinogen Drug Seizures ||
Year	Hallucinogen dosage units
2009	2,954,251
2008	9,199,693
2007	5,636,305
2006	4,606,277
2005	8,881,321
2004	2,261,706
2003	2,878,594
2002	11,661,157
2001	13,755,390
2000	29,307,427
1999	1,736,077
1998	1,075,457
1997	1,100,912
1996	1,719,209
1995	2,768,165
1994	1,366,817
1993	2,710,063
1992	1,305,177
1991	1,297,394
1990	2,826,966
1989	13,125,010
1988	16,706,442
1987	6,556,891
1986	4,146,329

Note: Calendar year 2000 had several large LSD seizures.
Source: U.S. Drug Enforcement Administration, http://
www.justice.gov/dea/statistics.html.

of the act was to create a single unified system for controlling both narcotics and psychedelics.

Perhaps the most important result of the CSA was the creation of a national list of narcotics and dangerous drugs that are federally controlled. The possession and trafficking of these drugs are strictly monitored by the federal government. The Controlled Substances List categorizes the most dangerous drugs into five "schedules" based on their danger to health, abuse potential, and medical uses. In general, the potential for abuse and penalties decrease from Schedule I through Schedule V.

Another critical ramification of the CSA, and part of President Nixon's "war on drugs," was the creation of the Drug Enforcement Agency (DEA). At the time, one of the major impediments to confronting the drug problem was the lack of coordination between various agencies, including the U.S. Customs Service and many local drug enforcement units, like the New York Drug Enforcement Task Force. Largely solving this problem, the new DEA had broad authority to oversee the nation's drug policy and was given the authority to coordinate activities between all enforcement agencies.

THE LEGAL HISTORY OF HALLUCINOGENS

Though synthetic hallucinogens were a relatively new class of drugs, legal actions against them began as early as the mid- to late-1960s. At the time, the DEA observed the following:

> Although initial observations of the benefits of LSD were highly optimistic, empirical data developed subsequently proved less promising. Its use in scientific research has been extensive and its use has been widespread. Although the study of LSD and other hallucinogens increased the awareness of how chemicals could affect the mind, its use in psychotherapy largely has been debunked. It produces aphrodisiac effects, does not increase creativity, has no lasting positive effect in treating alcoholics or criminals, does not produce a "model psychosis," and does not generate immediate personality change. Drug studies have confirmed, however, that the powerful hallucinogenic effects of this drug can produce profound adverse reactions, such as acute panic reactions, psychotic crises, and "flashbacks," especially in users who are ill-equipped to deal with such trauma.[3]

Similarly, the United Nations Economic and Social Council (UNESC) grew concerned with the rise of hallucinogen use, passing a resolution in 1968, calling on member nations to limit the use of these drugs to medical and scientific purposes. The UNESC was calling on nations worldwide to tighten legal restrictions over these substances within each country's legal framework. In the United States, with the implementation of the Controlled Substances Act (CSA) in 1971, LSD and most other hallucinogens were classified as Schedule I drugs. This meant that hallucinogens became illegal to manufacture, produce, purchase, possess, or distribute. The basic move to make psychedelic substances illegal expanded worldwide with the United Nation's signing of the Convention on Psychotropic Substances on February 21, 1971. The United Nations, which had already signed the Single Convention on Narcotic Drugs in 1961, recognized that a new treaty was required to deal with these new substances that did not fall under previous international law or control. Thus while the Single Convention was limited to drugs with opium-like effects, such as cannabis and coca, the new treaty brought the psychoactive drugs (amphetamines, barbiturates, benzodiazepines, and psychedelics) under international law. Specifically, the treaty limited the use of the active substances used to create most of the psychedelics, to medical research only. Import and export of the raw materials to make hallucinogens became highly restricted and regulated. Today 175 nations have signed on to the treaty.

MESCALINE: LEGAL ISSUES

In the United States, mescaline was made illegal by the passing of the CSA and was outlawed internationally by the Convention on Psychotropic Substances in 1971. Like LSD, mescaline is categorized as a Schedule I drug by the DEA. Certain religious groups, however, such as the Native American Church, are legally allowed to use mescaline in religious ceremonies for religious purposes. Through a series for court challenges, this legal use of mescaline was made illegal for a time, but the Supreme Court finally ruled that the federal government could not restrict the drug's use by Native American religious groups. As it stands today, individual states may impose their own restrictions. In the United Kingdom, mescaline in powder form is listed as a Class A drug and is illegal, although dried cactus may be bought or sold legally. Likewise, in Canada, mescaline in raw form is illegal, but as a plant, in the form of peyote, it is legal.

Figure 6.1 A 2010 drug seizure included 700,000 Ecstasy tablets. Ecstasy is a Schedule I drug under the Controlled Substances Act. *(© AP Images)*

PSILOCYBIN: LEGAL ISSUES

In the late 1960s, several laws were enacted in the United States to limit the legal use of psilocybin and psilocin. More specifically, psilocybin and psilocin were banned on October 24, 1968. Further, like other hallucinogens, they were classified as Schedule I substances by the CSA. Likewise possession and use of psilocybin and psilocin are similarly restricted in Canada, Europe, and the United Kingdom. That said, there seems to be a general lessening of enforcement of these restrictions in recent years.

KETAMINE: LEGAL ISSUES

Primarily used as an anesthetic in veterinary medicine, ketamine has also been used as an anesthetic for humans. With an increase in recreational use in the late 1990s, ketamine was added to the list of controlled substances in 1999, as a Schedule III narcotic. As a result, ketamine can only be used by health professionals or obtained with a prescription.

MDMA: LEGAL ISSUES

MDMA, otherwise known as Ecstasy, was made illegal in the United States on May 31, 1985. At that time, Ecstasy was listed as a Schedule I drug, carrying significant penalties for manufacture, possession, and sale. Nevertheless some critics contend that MDMA has legitimate use for medical purposes and thus should be classified as a Schedule III drug.

HALLUCINOGEN PENALTIES

The federal penalties for trafficking (sale) of hallucinogens are on par with those penalties for other drugs like cocaine and heroin. More specifically, as Schedule I substances, LSD, psilocybin, and mescaline carry a trafficking penalty for a first offense of no less than five years in prison with a maximum of 40 years, a maximum fine of $2 million, or both. For trafficking of Schedule III substances like MDMA and ketamine, there is a maximum of five years in prison, a fine of not more than $250,000, or both. Beyond this, it is common for each individual state to lay out more specific penalties for trafficking and additional penalties for possession and use. For example, in Connecticut, possession of 4 ounces of any hallucinogen comes with a first offense penalty of up to a five-year jail term, and up to a $2,000 fine. According to the law, subsequent offenses carry a potential 10-year jail sentence and up to a $5,000 fine. A first offense penalty in Connecticut for the sale of hallucinogens carries a maximum 15-year imprisonment, a $50,000 fine, or both; subsequent offenses carry a 30-year prison term, a $100,000 fine, or both.[4] Generally speaking, penalties for possession or use of small amounts of controlled substances are less severe than trafficking penalties.

7
Club Drugs

It was Friday night and Jen was just about ready to go. Her best friend, Sarah, told her about a party that she claimed would last all night. At first Jen thought it was strange that they were starting so late, looking at the clock and seeing that it was already well after midnight. After what seemed like a very long drive, down some back roads that Jen wasn't familiar with, they finally arrived at an old warehouse. As she stepped out of the car, Jen could hear the pounding music from inside the large building. She couldn't believe how crowded it was, with what seemed like a thousand people dancing. Almost immediately a guy approached her from the bar and handed her a drink; he said it was a gin and tonic. After she finished the drink, Jen immediately felt more relaxed and the music didn't seem as loud. She started to dance with the guy who'd bought her the drink and she felt full of energy and love. The next thing she knew it was morning. It was cold, even with the light streaming through the window of the car. Sitting up, Jen realized that she wasn't in the same car she arrived in; Sarah was nowhere to be seen. Next to her, still asleep in the car, was the guy she'd danced with earlier in the night. She was suddenly very frightened: She couldn't remember anything after drinking that first drink. She put on her clothes and set out to find Sarah, very confused and very scared, realizing now that her drink had been spiked and she had experienced temporary amnesia.

LSD hit its high-water mark in terms of use in the 1960s and 1970s, but the late 1990s ushered in a new trend in hallucinogen use. Two drugs, MDMA (commonly known as Ecstasy or simply as *E*) and ketamine experienced a rapid rise in use as they became intertwined with a burgeoning "rave" culture. In popular nomenclature, a rave is similar to a club environment, only on a grander scale. Raves began in the late-20th century as a rural phenomenon, often held in secret locations, typically in large warehouses. With loud, heart-pounding music and extravagant light shows, these rave parties typically started late at night and proceeded until dawn. Raves have recently become more mainstream, occurring in legitimate clubs or large rented spaces in urban areas. Wherever the location, the use of Ecstasy and ketamine quickly caught on as the principal substances used at raves, clubs, and techno concerts.

Between the two, Ecstasy is the more popular drug used at these functions. Associated with warm, empathetic feelings, and low-level "visuals" or mild hallucinations, participants view an Ecstasy experience as a way to more deeply connect with the music, space, and other ravers. Users of Ecstasy often report a lessoning in feelings of shyness, an easing of communication with others. Feelings of depression fade away and users often feel as if all is right

Figure 7.1 There are many drugs used in the club scene, but Ecstasy and ketamine are two popular hallucinogenic club drugs. (© *shutterstock*)

with the world. Put another way, users are left without a care or concern, and find themselves only able to focus on the present experience, whatever or wherever that may be. One raver described the experience as follows:

> A wave of warmth overcame me on my way down. For the first time in my life, I knew what empathy felt like. I thought that everyone was my friend, simply due to the fact that those around me (even if I didn't know them) shared and enhanced this feeling just by being around me. The world seemed like a better place. There was no war, no poverty, no pain while I was rolling. I never felt closer to my friends who were there until then also. We were sharing something that we all knew the others were feeling. We were all in tune with each other's thoughts, feelings, emotions.[1]

THE PHYSICAL EFFECTS OF ECSTASY AND KETAMINE

For those who abuse Ecstasy, it is commonly believed that there are only positive physical effects, but in fact, Ecstasy is a very dangerous drug with serious negative consequences. Users believe that the drug will allow them to be more social, more awake, and have more fun. In terms of chemical structure, Ecstasy shows similarities to cocaine, but with the addition of hallucinogenic chemical properties. Most hallucinogens work by blocking the re-uptake of serotonin in the brain, which in turn causes a buildup of serotonin, ultimately imparting its psychoactive effects. But Ecstasy works a little differently; instead of blocking the re-uptake of serotonin, Ecstasy actually causes the brain to release stores of serotonin so there is an overall increase in serotonin levels throughout the brain.

While increased levels of serotonin may indeed create a temporary sense of well-being, often lasting for several hours, and while Ecstasy's amphetamine-like attributes will create an increase in energy and the ability to stay awake for extended periods of time, there are also a host of negative effects. Many users of the drug experience dryness of the mouth; some also report increased heart rate, eye twitching, blurred vision, sweating, and nausea. Longer, lasting effects include confusion, sleep problems, anxiety, an acne-like rash, jaw clenching, teeth grinding, depression, aggression, and liver and brain damage.

WHAT IS KETAMINE?

Ketamine is an anesthetic that is abused for its hallucinogenic properties. Its predominant legitimate use is as a veterinary anesthetic; however, it has been approved for use with both animals and humans. Abuse of the drug gained popularity when users discovered that it produced effects similar to those associated with PCP. Because of its anesthetic properties, ketamine also reportedly has been used by sexual predators to incapacitate their intended victims.

What does ketamine look like?
Ketamine generally is sold as either a colorless, odorless liquid or as a white or off-white powder.

How is ketamine used?
In either its powder or liquid forms, ketamine is mixed with beverages or added to smokable materials such as marijuana or tobacco. As a powder the drug is snorted or pressed into tablets—often in combination with other drugs such as 3,4-methylenedioxymethamphetamine (MDMA, also known as Ecstasy). As a liquid, ketamine is injected; it often is injected intramuscularly.

Who uses ketamine?
Teenagers and young adults represent the majority of ketamine users. According to the Drug Abuse Warning Network, individuals aged 12 to 25 accounted for 74% of the ketamine emergency department mentions in the United States in 2000.

Ketamine use among high school students is a particular concern. Nearly 3% of high school seniors in the United States used the drug at least once in the past year, according to the University of Michigan's Monitoring the Future Survey.

What are the risks of using ketamine?
Ketamine causes users to have distorted perceptions of sight and sound and to feel disconnected and out of control. Use of the drug can impair an individual's senses, judgment, and coordination for up to 24 hours after the drug is taken, even though the drug's hallucinogenic effects usually last for only 45 to 90 minutes.

(continues)

(continued)

Use of ketamine has been associated with serious problems—both mental and physical. Ketamine can cause depression, delirium, amnesia, impaired motor function, high blood pressure, and potentially fatal respiratory problems.

In addition to the risks associated with ketamine itself, individuals who use the drug may put themselves at risk of sexual assault. Sexual predators reportedly have used ketamine to incapacitate their intended victims—either by lacing unsuspecting victims' drinks with the drug or by offering ketamine to victims who consume the drug without understanding the effects it will produce.

Are there other names for ketamine?
The most common names for ketamine are K, Special K, cat valium, and Vitamin K.

Is ketamine illegal?
Yes, it is illegal to abuse ketamine. Ketamine is a controlled substance. Specifically, it is a Schedule III substance under the Controlled Substances Act. Schedule III drugs, which include codeine and anabolic steroids, have less potential for abuse than Schedule I (heroin) or Schedule II (cocaine) drugs. Abuse of Schedule III substances, however, may lead to physical or psychological dependence on the drug.

Source: U.S. Department of Justice, "Ketamine Fast Facts," http://www.justice.gov/ndic/pubs4/4769/index.htm.

Long-term use of Ecstasy, most often used by young adults, results in an overall lowering of serotonin and dopamine in the brain. This happens because the unnatural heightening of these chemicals through the use of Ecstasy creates falsely high levels for a time. Adjusting to this, the brain reduces normal output of these important chemicals, creating a new normal level. Thus, once the user stops taking the drug, the amount of these chemicals in the brain stays lower. Scientists who have studied the effect of Ecstasy on the brain indicate that significant brain damage can occur in some individuals. One study, for example, showed that in primates, exposure to MDMA for a four-day period caused brain damage that was evident six to seven years later.[2]

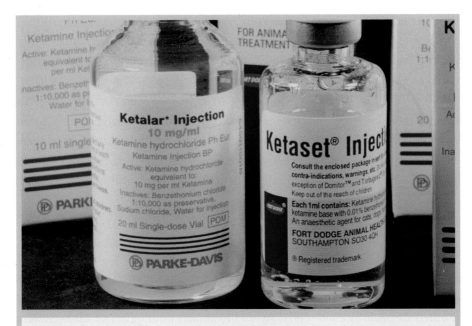

Figure 7.2 Ketamine works by binding to opioid receptors in the brain, which creates a dissociative state in the user. *(© Alamy)*

Ketamine, also referred to as Vitamin K or Special K, is an anesthetic drug that is used widely in veterinary medicine and in humans as well. More specifically, ketamine is used in cases of severe trauma, surgery, or in war zones. Because of its hallucinatory effects it is not used as a primary anesthetic. Ketamine has also been tested as a potential treatment for depression, though with limited success. In medical settings ketamine is delivered in liquid form as an injection. Ketamine was invented by Dr. Craig Newlands of Wayne State University and developed by the pharmaceutical company Parke-Davis in 1962, as a safer alternative to PCP. It was first used as an anesthetic, given to soldiers during the Vietnam War.

Because it has hallucinatory effects similar to PCP and LSD, ketamine has more recently, within the last 5–10 years, become popular as a recreational drug, especially within the club-rave scene. In this environment the drug is often mixed into drinks, added to other smokable materials, or snorted.

Ketamine works by binding to opioid receptors in the brain, which creates a dissociative state in the user. In small doses the drug can alleviate anxiety, intensify colors and sounds, and relieve pain; the drug is also purported to be a sexual stimulant. In the recreational setting, the use of ketamine is sometimes referred to as "K-land." At higher doses the drug causes more intense hallucinations, and an out-of-body experience, which is often compared to a near-death experience and referred to as the "K-hole."[3]

Ketamine use carries a wide range of negative side effects. Short-term effects include hypersalivation, nausea, sedation, hypertension, slowed breathing, lack of coordination, and slurred speech, among others. Longer-term use often results in more serious cognitive issues, such as amnesia and long-term memory loss, increased urination, addiction and other neuroses, and irreversible mental disorders.

THE USE OF ECSTASY AND KETAMINE

Ecstasy is taken as a capsule or tablet, often in conjunction with other substances, like cocaine, marijuana, even Viagra. The use of Ecstasy, or MDMA, reached its peak in 2000–2001. At that time just under 12% of 12th-graders reported using MDMA at least once. Recognizing the steep increase in prevalence of MDMA, the DEA increased its focus on the drug; the U.S. Customs Service seized 750,000 Ecstasy tablets in 1998, 3.5 million in 1999, and 9.3 million in 2000.[4] While the use of MDMA declined after the 2001 high-water mark, its use is starting to slowly increase, according to surveys conducted in recent years. The 2010 Monitoring the Future Survey found that

Table 7.1 MDMA Use by U.S. Students, 2010			
	8th Grade	10th Grade	12th Grade
Lifetime	3.3%	6.4%	7.3%
Past Year	2.4%	4.7%	4.5%
Past Month	1.1%	1.9%	1.4%

Note: "Lifetime" refers to use at least once during a respondent's lifetime. "Past year" refers to use at least once during the year preceding an individual's response to the survey. "Past month" refers to use at least once during the 30 days preceding an individual's response to the survey.
Source: National Institute on Drug Abuse, Monitoring the Future Survey 2010, http://www.drugabuse.gov/infofacts/ecstasy.html.

7.3% of 12th-graders had used MDMA at some point during their lifetime, 4.5% had used in the past year, and 1.4% had done so in the past month.

According the National Survey on Drug Use and Health (NSDUH), in 2009, approximately 760,000 people, or 0.3% of the U.S. population, over 12 years old used MDMA in the month prior to the survey. Lifetime use increased significantly among individuals aged 12 years or older, from 4.3% (10.2 million) in 2002, to 5.7% (14.2 million) in 2009; however, past-year use of Ecstasy decreased from 1.3% to 1.1% during the same period.[5] Overall, the study found that 1.1 million Americans used MDMA for the first time in 2009, which constituted a major increase, from 894,000, in 2008.

Ketamine, a Schedule III drug under the Controlled Substances Act, is produced commercially in a number of countries; however, the National Drug Intelligence Center reports that most illicit ketamine in the United States is of Mexican origin.[6] In fact, it is believed that as much as 80% of illegal ketamine

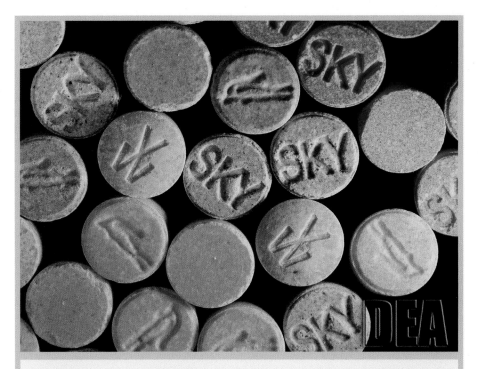

Figure 7.3 Long-term use of Ecstasy results in an overall lowering of serotonin and dopamine in the brain.

WHAT IS ECSTASY?

Ecstasy (3, 4-methylenedioxy-N-methylamphetamine, or MDMA) is a drug that is illegally made. Ecstasy is a stimulant that can cause hallucinations. It is known as a designer drug because it is created for the purpose of making someone feel high. The drug is popular with teens and young adults who go to clubs, concerts, or "rave parties." Users think the drug will make them feel good and enable them to keep going for days without rest. But people who use Ecstasy don't realize how dangerous this drug actually is.

Ecstasy has become one of the most common illegal drugs sold on the streets. In the last few years, Ecstasy has sent many young people to emergency rooms because of its dangerous side effects. Ecstasy can kill. Ecstasy is sometimes called: XTC, X, Adam, E, Roll, A, and 007.

How is Ecstasy used?
Ecstasy can be swallowed (pill or tablet) or snorted (powder).

What does Ecstasy do?
Ecstasy is both a hallucinogenic and a stimulant drug. It makes users experience a rush of good feelings (a high) and makes someone's feelings much more intense, whether good or bad. The drug's effects usually last up to six hours.

Ecstasy increases heart rate and can cause dry mouth, stomach cramps, blurred vision, chills, sweating, or nausea. It can make some users feel anxious, confused, and paranoid, like someone is trying to hurt them or is plotting against them. Scientists have recently proven that Ecstasy causes direct damage to brain cells that are involved in thinking and memory.

The drug can cause the salts and minerals in the blood to become dangerously diluted (thinned out), which can cause the brain to swell. Permanent brain damage can result.

If a person takes Ecstasy, his body can dangerously overheat during dancing or other physical activities, which can lead to death.

Source: KidsHealth, "What You Need to Know About Drugs: Ecstasy," http://kidshealth.org/kid/grow/drugs_alcohol/know_drugs_ecstasy.html.

is smuggled into the United States from Mexico. The DEA has found that most ketamine is sold by Caucasian males aged 17–25, and consumed by teenagers and young adults. Typically the point of sale is a nightclub or rave situation; street sales are relatively limited.

According to the 2008 Monitoring the Future Report, the annual prevalence of ketamine among 8th-, 10th- and 12th-graders is 1.2%, 1.0%, and 1.5%, respectively. These figures are on par with those for MDMA, which is not surprising given that these drugs are often taken in combination or by the same individuals. Usage statistics for ketamine (Note: these stats are indicated above) did not change significantly when compared to the previous year, which showed an annual prevalence of 1.0% use among 8th-graders, 0.8% of 10th-graders, and 1.3% of 12th-graders. Further, according to the NSDUH study, an estimated 2.3 million persons aged 12 or older used ketamine in their lifetime in 2006, and 203,000 were past-year users.[7]

One of the biggest concerns regarding the use of ketamine is its use as a potential "date rape" drug. Because ketamine is tasteless and odorless as a powder, it can easily be slipped into a drink and consumed without a person's knowledge. Once consumed, the user may experience temporary amnesia and a general numbness wherein they have difficulty recalling events. In addition to this, the greatest danger involving ketamine use is when it is mixed with other substances. For example, users often engage in a practice termed "rolling," in which they mix combinations of drugs to see what will happen. The combination of cocaine and ketamine is particularly popular, but also extremely dangerous, not to mention that the use of alcohol at parties and raves is quite ubiquitous. It is this practice of mixing drugs that most often results in drug-related deaths or visits to the emergency room.

8

Looking Ahead: Designer Drugs and Research Chemicals

Having conducted surveillance of the underground drug laboratory, the local police knew that something was up. Based on an anonymous tip about strange smells emanating from a local warehouse, two officers were assigned to stake out the location; they suspected that it was some type of illegal drug laboratory. A spike in hallucinogen use in prior months also led them to believe that the lab was indeed producing hallucinogens. With enough evidence to obtain a warrant and search the facility, the officers entered the lab without prior warning. From a quick look around, it seemed that the police had been correct and some form of illegal drug was being produced. They saw all of the classic indicators, such as the makeshift lab equipment and lab books detailing processes for the manufacture of LSD. After they made arrests and confiscated the equipment and drug powder, the police sent a sample of the powder, which they believed to be ergotamine tartrate, the raw material needed to manufacture LSD, to the local forensics laboratory. When the test results came in, the officers were very surprised to discover that this wasn't ergotamine tartrate at all. Instead, the results indicated that this was ETH-LAD, a manipulated form of LSD that, while chemically different, results in similar LSD-like effects. It was only then that they realized they'd uncovered a designer drug laboratory.

Naturally occurring hallucinogens like psilocybin mushrooms and peyote have been used for thousands of years. These were typically used for ceremonial or religious purposes; their use continues in this fashion among Native Americans to this day. In the United States, as early as the 1950s, synthetic

RECAP: POPULAR HALLUCINOGEN DRUGS

LSD—Lysergic acid diethylamide-25 is the full name for LSD, a synthetic chemical derived from ergot, a toxic mold that grows on rye. Commonly referred to as acid, sunshine, and windowpane, LSD is most often distributed via impregnated paper, tablets, sugar cubes, and occasionally in liquid form. The effects of LSD include dilated pupils, reduced body temperature, sweating, nausea, and increased heart rate, among others. The psychedelic effects of LSD cause the user to hear sounds and see colors, and experience an altered sense of time; these effects can last as long as 12 hours. While long-term effects remain a subject of great debate, it is probable that some types of long-term mental health conditions are associated with the drug's frequent use at a young age.

Psilocybin—Psilocybin is part of a group of chemicals known as tryptamines and is found as a natural ingredient in certain species of mushrooms that grow primarily in South America, Mexico, and the United States. The substance is most commonly referred to as "magic mushrooms," and while most often taken in its natural form, it can also be ground into tablets. The effects of magic mushrooms are very similar to LSD but less predictable, both in terms of intensity and time.

Peyote—Peyote comes from certain species of cacti including *Lophophora williamsii* and *Lophophora lewinii*. These cacti grow close to the ground and are commonly referred to as "buttons." These buttons are soaked in water to produce an intoxicating liquid. The active ingredient in the plant, which causes hallucinatory effects, is called mescaline. The use of peyote often begins with severe nausea and vomiting, followed by a long (12-hour) high in which there are expansive mood swings, visualizations, and out-of-body experiences.

hallucinogens like LSD became extremely popular. First discovered in a pharmaceutical laboratory, LSD quickly became the most popular hallucinogen of its time, and remains a significant player in today's drug culture. Popularized in the 1960s through its association with rock music, artists, and popular culture in general, LSD was eventually overshadowed in part by cocaine and heroin in the 1970s and 1980s. More recently, combination or "designer" hallucinogens like Ecstasy burst onto the scene. Because Ecstasy contains both hallucinatory and amphetamine-like qualities, it was particularly well suited for the rave scene, in which participants dance to loud techno music for extended periods of time.

Having slowed in the late-20th century, the use of hallucinogens continues as a trend today, and newer substances like PCP are, unfortunately, increasing in use. In search of new types of hallucinatory experiences, some users experiment with other extremely dangerous substances as well, such as **jimsonweed.**

Phencyclidine (PCP) was invented in 1959, and used as a veterinary anesthetic. Through the 1960s to 1980s, the drug enjoyed limited popularity among people using other hallucinogens. But the drug did not become as popular as other hallucinogens, most likely due to the bizarre type of hallucinations or frequent "bad trips" that it causes. Typically, users of this drug experience loss of coordination, convulsions, terrifying flashbacks, and often exhibit violent behavior. Many motiveless crimes have been the result of abuse of PCP. Because of the drug's severe negative consequences, it was discontinued as a veterinary anesthetic in 1978. PCP has demonstrated somewhat of a comeback in recent years. The comeback of the drug has been connected to the shift of rave culture to the suburbs. Confiscating drugs from rave parties, law enforcement officials were initially shocked to find that PCP was emerging once again. Most disconcerting is the fact that trace amounts of PCP turn up in pills of Ecstasy; thus the Ecstasy user may take PCP without ever knowing.

PCP is also referred to as angel dust, rocket fuel, and ozone. It has also been called embalming fluid because it can often leave the user in a catatonic state. The drug most commonly appears in the form of a powder or liquid, which is applied to a cigarette or marijuana and smoked. The effects of PCP most often include numbness, slurred speech, uncoordination, and visual and auditory distortions. Most of all, the drug seems to be abused by those seeking a total break from the real world. Studies indicate that extended use of PCP can lead to long-term brain damage. With all of its negative consequences, the drug's rising use begs the question: Why is it increasing in popularity? So far,

WHAT IS 2 C-B?

One hallucinogen that we have not focused on at length is called 2 C-B. 2 C-B (4-bromo-2, 5-dimethoxyhenethylamine) is a synthetic hallucinogen similar to LSD. It is known for the strong physical component of its effects. 2 C-B is considered gentler than LSD or mushrooms, and users report being less prone to "freak-outs," overwhelming panic attacks at normal recreational doses.

How is 2 C-B used?
2 C-B is most often found in either powder or pill form. It normally takes 45 to 75 minutes to take effect. The primary effects of 2 C-B generally last four to six hours.

How does 2 C-B work?
At the beginning stages of onset, 2 C-B is likely to cause anticipation and anxiety. At lower doses (5–15 mg), it produces entactogenic effects, with little or no hallucinations. Users feel "in touch" with themselves and their emotions. Erotic sensations and feelings of being "in one's body" have also been reported. 2 C-B seems to produce "pleasurable energy." At higher doses (15–30 mg), 2 C-B produces intense visual effects, such as moving objects leaving trails behind them, surfaces covered with geometric patterns that may appear to be moving or breathing, and colors that seem to appear from nowhere.

What are 2 C-B's side effects?
As reported above, perceptual changes often occur as do pupil dilation, visual patterning and movement, mental stimulation, new perspectives, feelings of insight, emotional shifts, and/or anxiety and confusion. Open-eye visual patterning, color shift, and wavering or moving vision are common for many people and more likely at higher doses. Unpleasant stomach effects, allergic type reactions, and unwanted thoughts or visions are also possible.

Source: Institute for Substance Abuse Treatment Evaluation, "Hallucinogen," http://www.isate.memphis.edu/hallucinogen.html.

WHAT IS PCP?

PCP (phencyclidine) was developed in the 1950s as an intravenous anesthetic, but its use for humans was discontinued because it caused patients to become agitated, delusional, and irrational. Today, individuals abuse PCP because of the mind-altering, hallucinogenic effects it produces.

What does PCP look like?
PCP is a bitter-tasting, white crystalline powder that is easy to dissolve in water or alcohol. PCP may be dyed various colors and often is sold as a tablet, capsule, liquid, or powder.

How is PCP used?
Users snort PCP powder, swallow tablets and capsules, or smoke the drug by applying it (in powder form) to a leafy substance such as marijuana, mint, parsley, or oregano. In addition, users increasingly are dipping marijuana or tobacco cigarettes in liquid PCP and smoking them.

Who uses PCP?
Individuals of all ages use PCP. Data reported in the National Household Survey on Drug Abuse indicate that an estimated 6 million U.S. residents aged 12 and older used PCP at least once in their lifetime.

The survey also revealed that many teenagers and young adults use PCP—225,000 individuals aged 12 to 17 and 777,000 individuals aged 18 to 25 used the drug at least once. PCP use among high school students is a particular concern. More than 3% of high school seniors in the United States used the drug at least once in their lifetime, and more than 1% used the drug in the past year, according to the University of Michigan's Monitoring the Future Survey.

the only answer experts have been able to surmise is that PCP is cheaper than other comparable drugs.

Another drug that has sprung up in recent times is called jimsonweed, more technically known as *Datura stramonium*. Like peyote and psilocybin, jimsonweed is a natural plant that has hallucinogenic properties. As a result, also like peyote and psilocybin, it has been used for thousands of years. But

What are the risks of using PCP?
PCP is an addictive drug; its use often results in psychological dependence, craving, and compulsive behavior. PCP produces unpleasant psychological effects, and users often become violent or suicidal.

PCP poses particular risks for young people. Even moderate use of the drug can negatively affect the hormones associated with normal growth and development. PCP use also can impede the learning process in teenagers.

High doses of PCP can cause seizures, coma, and even death (often as a consequence of accidental injury or suicide while under the drug's effects). At high doses PCP's effects may resemble the symptoms associated with schizophrenia, including delusions and paranoia. Long-term use of PCP can lead to memory loss, difficulty with speech or thought, depression, and weight loss. These problems can persist for up to a year after an individual has stopped using PCP.

Are there other names for PCP?
The most common names for PCP are angel dust, animal tranquilizer, embalming fluid, ozone, rocket fuel, and wack. Marijuana or tobacco cigarettes that are dipped in PCP are called illy, wet, or fry.

Is PCP illegal?
Yes, PCP is illegal. PCP is a Schedule II substance under the Controlled Substances Act. Schedule II drugs, which include cocaine and methamphetamine, have a high potential for abuse. Abuse of these drugs may lead to severe psychological or physical dependence.

Source: U.S. Department of Justice, "PCP Fast Facts," http://www.justice.gov/ndic/pubs4/4440/index.htm.

similar to PCP, it is surprising that this lethal substance is currently still used today. The plant's main ingredients are the belladonna alkaloids **atropine** and **scopolamine**, and it is native to the United States. As a result, young people familiar with the drug's hallucinatory reputation often consume it without understanding the deadly consequences. Also referred to as thorn apple, stinkweed, and locoweed, the plant grows as tall as five feet and has white flowers when in bloom. The effects of the plant when consumed include dry mouth, dilated pupils, high temperature, and blurred vision.

These effects result from the fact that atropine and scopolamine block the neurotransmitter *acetylcholine*. At high doses the drug causes intense sensory distortions, seizures, cardiac arrest, and death. Jimsonweed is not listed as a controlled substance by the DEA and thus does not fall under any U.S. drug laws. Typically speaking, most cases of jimsonweed use stem from young adventure seekers, curious about the effects of the drug. Jimsonweed should be viewed, however, for what it really is: a poisonous plant.

DESIGNER DRUGS

The term *designer drugs* was first coined by the DEA in the 1980s. It refers to drugs that are essentially tweaks of existing illegal drugs. Typically the creators of these so-called designer drugs change the chemical structure of a narcotic compound, creating an *analogue*, which is intended to have the same narcotic properties as the drug it is designed to mimic. In rare cases a completely new drug is developed to mimic a current drug, with a completely different molecular structure. These analogues are created to avoid the controlled substance laws as they are often, at least initially, not listed as illegal drugs. It is these types of drugs that, particularly in the case of hallucinogens, represent the future of the drug class.

While new designer drugs are continuously crafted today, the first examples of this practice of manipulating illegal drugs date back to the 1920s, following the passage of the International Opium Convention in 1925. Shortly after the implementation of the law, subversive scientists began to toy around with and create analogues of morphine and heroin, forcing officials to ban these subsequent substances. After LSD was banned, a similar pattern emerged and through the 1970s, a number of synthetic LSD-like drugs were produced. Likewise, in the 1980s and 1990s, designer forms of PCP and MDMA emerged, continuing the perpetual cat and mouse game between the creation of new hallucinogens and the ability of the DEA to place them under legal control.

In the early-21st century there was an explosion of the sale of designer drugs through the Internet. New companies were set up and avoided applicable laws by creating products which they referred to as "research chemicals." Most of these experimental chemicals were analogues (compounds with similar molecular structures) of well-known hallucinogens like mescaline and psilocybin. Typically these so-called research chemicals were manufactured in powdered form, as manufacturing into pill form would negate the "research" aspect of their legal argument. As a result, many emergency rooms visits resulted from users getting hold of these chemicals and taking them in too-large dosages.

The continual crackdown on new designer drugs and research chemicals has not eliminated public use. Today, the general trend is toward the creation of new and often combination type products, for example, combining a stimulant with a hallucinogen. And while the legal status of these new drugs was intended to fall under the Controlled Substance Analogue Enforcement Act of 1986, officials have had trouble controlling the stream of new products. As a result, these chemical products are most often placed under government control on a piecemeal basis.

LOOKING AHEAD

The use of hallucinogens may never be eradicated fully, and the creation of new designer hallucinogen drugs shows that there remains high demand for these kinds of drugs. However, the use of hallucinogens when compared to other drug categories, such as opiates, remains relatively small. People who do experiment with hallucinogens, whether the drugs are new or old, natural or synthetic, powder or pill, should do so with the knowledge that they may be putting their life on the line. While some, it seems, are willing to take this risk in order to achieve a temporary high or disassociation from the real world, most people are unwilling to make this potentially deadly wager.

Appendix: Chronology: LSD

November 16, 1938	Albert Hofmann, a chemist working for Sandoz Pharmaceutical in Basel, Switzerland, is the first to synthesize LSD-25. He discovers LSD, a semi-synthetic derivative of ergot alkaloids, while looking for a blood stimulant.
April 16, 1943	Albert Hofmann accidentally experiences a small amount of LSD for the first time. This is the first human experience with pure LSD-25. He reports seeing "an uninterrupted stream of fantastic pictures, extraordinary shapes with intense, kaleidoscope-like play of colors." The experience lasts just over two hours.
April 19, 1943	Albert Hofmann intentionally takes (250 ug) LSD for the first time. This is the first intentional use of LSD.
1947	The first article on LSD's mental effects is published by Werner Stoll in the *Swiss Archives of Neurology*.
1949	Dr. Max Rinkel brings LSD to the United States from Sandoz Pharmaceuticals in Switzerland, and initiates work with LSD in Boston; Nick Bercel commences LSD study in Los Angeles.
1950–1960	Hundreds of papers are published discussing LSD.
May 1950	The first article about LSD appears in the *American Psychiatric Journal*.
1951	The CIA becomes aware of and begins experimenting with LSD. Al Hubbard, a notable early proponent of the drug, first tries LSD.

1953	The first LSD clinic opens to the public in England under Ronald Sandison, a British psychiatrist well known for early exploration of LSD's clinical usages. Dr. Humphrey Osmond, a British psychiatrist who invented the term *psychedelic*, begins treating alcoholics with LSD. Separately, unwitting subjects in the United States are given LSD in the CIA-funded Project MK-ULTRA to test the effects of the drug.
1955	The first conferences focusing on LSD and mescaline take place in Atlantic City and Princeton, N.J. Writer Aldous Huxley first takes LSD; his novel *Heaven and Hell* is published.
1959	Josiah Macy Foundation sponsors major scientific congress on LSD. Poet Allen Ginsberg tries LSD for the first time.
1960	Harvard University's Timothy Leary establishes the Psilocybin Research Project.
1962	Congress passes new drug-safety regulations and the FDA designates LSD an experimental drug and restricts research. The first LSD-related arrests are made.
1963	LSD first appears on the streets (as a liquid on sugar cubes). Articles about LSD first appear in mainstream media (*Look, Saturday Evening Post*).
May 1963	Timothy Leary and Richard Alpert are fired from Harvard.
February 1965	Owsley "Bear" Stanley first succeeded in synthesizing crystalline LSD. Earliest distribution was March 1965.
1966	Leary founds the League for Spiritual Development, with LSD as the sacrament.
March 25, 1966	*Life* publishes cover article on LSD. "LSD: The Exploding Threat of the Mind Drug that Got Out of Control."

April 1966	Sandoz Pharmaceutical recalls the LSD it had previously distributed and withdraws its sponsorship of work involving LSD.
October 6, 1966	LSD becomes illegal in California.
October 24, 1968	Possession of LSD is banned federally in the United States after the passage of the Staggers-Dodd Bill (Public Law 90–639), which amends the Food, Drug, and Cosmetic Act.
Summer 1969	Orange sunshine acid, the first largely available form of LSD, first appears.
1970	It is estimated that 102 million Americans have used LSD.
June 1970	Windowpane acid (gelatin squares) first reported by the Bureau of Narcotics and Dangerous Drugs in the United States.
October 27, 1970	The Comprehensive Drug Abuse Prevention and Control Act is passed. Part II of this is the Controlled Substances Act (CSA), which defines a scheduling system for drugs. It places most of the known hallucinogens (LSD, psilocybin, psilocin, mescaline, peyote, and MDMA) in Schedule I.
Early 1970s	LSD impregnated paper ("blotter") first hits the streets. Very quickly the paper is printed with colorful art.
Mid 1970s	Blotter paper begins to emerge as the most common form of LSD sold on the street. Previously it had been tablets and powder, but blotter and gel-tabs proved more consistent in purity and potency.
1979	Albert Hofmann publishes *LSD: My Problem Child*.
April 29, 2008	Albert Hofmann dies.

Sources: Martin A. Lee and Bruce Shlain, *Acid Dreams, The Complete Social History of LSD: The CIA, the Sixties, and Beyond.* New York: Grove Press, 1985; Clayton James Mosher and Scott Akins, *Drugs and Drug Policy: The Control of Consciousness Alteration.* Thousand Oaks, Cal.: Sage Publications, 2006.

Notes

Chapter 1

1 James Barter, *Hallucinogens* (San Diego: Lucent Books, 2002).
2 Institute for Substance Abuse Treatment Evaluation, "Hallucinogen," http://www.isate .memphis.edu/hallucinogen. html (accessed June 13, 2011).
3 DrugPolicy.org, "Psychedelics," http://www.drugpolicy.org/ facts/drug-facts/salvia-and -psychedelics (accessed June 13, 2011).
4 Ibid.
5 About.com, "What Are Dissociative Drugs?," http://alcoholism .about.com/cs/lsd/f/lsd_faq02 .htm?p=1 (accessed June 11, 2011).
6 Drugs-Forum.com, "Deliriants," http://www.drugs-forum.com/ forum/showwiki.php?title= Category:Deliriants (accessed June 13, 2011).
7 National Institute on Drug Abuse, "NIDA InfoFacts: Hallucinogens–LSD, Peyote, Psilocybin, and PCP," http:// www.nida.nih.gov/infofacts/ hallucinogens.html (accessed June 13, 2011).
8 U.S. Drug Enforcement Administration, "Hallucinogens," http://www.justice.gov/dea/ concern/hallucinogens.html (accessed June 13, 2011).

Chapter 2

1 James Barter, *Hallucinogens* (San Diego: Lucent Books, 2002).
2 Drug Information Resource. com,"Magic Mushroom Facts," http://www.drug-information- resource.com/magic_ mushrooms_cont.html (accessed June 13, 2011).
3 James Barter, *Hallucinogens* (San Diego: Lucent Books, 2002).
4 Albert Hofmann, *LSD, My Problem Child,* trans. Jonathan Ott (New York: McGraw-Hill, 1980), 28.
5 Mary E. Williams, *Hallucinogens* (Farmington Hills, Mich.: Greenhaven Press, 2005).
6 *Newsweek,* "Droupouts with a Mission" (February 6, 1967) 92, 95.

Chapter 3

1 The Good Drugs Guide.com, "Types of Hallucinogens," http://www.thegooddrugsguide .com/drug-types/types-of-hallucinogens.htm (accessed June 14, 2011).

2 University of Bristol School of Chemistry, "Lysergic Acid Diethylamide," http://www .chm.bris.ac.uk/motm/ serotonin/LSD.HTM (accessed June 14, 2011).

3 Schaffer Library of Drug Policy, "LSD Manufacture," http:// www.druglibrary.org/schaffer/ dea/pubs/lsd/LSD-5 .htm (accessed June 14, 2011).

4 Anonymous, *Go Ask Alice* (New York: Aladdin Paperbacks, 1971).

5 Gerald D. Klee, "Clinical Studies with LSD-25 and Two Substances Related to Serotonin," *Journal of Mental Science* (1960) 106: 301–308.

6 William McGlothlin and David O. Arnold, "LSD Revisited—A Ten-Year Follow-up of Medical LSD Use," *Archives of General Psychiatry* 24 (January 1971): 35–49.

7 Stephen J. Kish, "What Is the Evidence That Ecstasy (MDMA) Can Cause Parkinson's Disease?," *Movement Disorders* 18, no. 11 (2003): 1219–1223.

Chapter 4

1 Los Angeles Police Department Drug Recognition Expert Unit, "Hallucinogens," http://www .ci.la.ca.us/LAPD/traffic/dre/ halluc.htm (accessed May 30, 2011).

2 Ibid.

3 Substance Abuse and Mental Health Services Administration, "Use of Specific Hallucinogens: 2006," National Survey on Drug Use and Health Report. http://www.oas.samhsa .gov/2k8/hallucinogens/ hallucinogens.cfm (accessed May 30, 2011).

4 National Institute on Drug Abuse, "NIDA InfoFacts: Hallucinogens–LSD, Peyote, Psilocybin, and PCP," http:// www.nida.nih.gov/infofacts/ hallucinogens.html (accessed May 30, 2011).

Chapter 5

1 Institute for Substance Abuse Treatment Evaluation, "Hallucinogen," http://www.isate .memphis.edu/hallucinogen .html (accessed June 14, 2011).

2 Emedicine.medscape.com, "Hallucinogens," http:// emedicine.medscape.com/ article/293752-print (accessed May 30, 2011).

3 Narcotics Anonymous, "Narcotics Anonymous, White Booklet," http://www.na.org/admin/include/spaw2/uploads/pdf/litfiles/us_english/Booklet/NA%20White%20Booklet.pdf (accessed June 14, 2011).

4 Passaic County Area of Narcotics Anonymous, "Narcotics Anonymous," http://www.passaicarea.org/Facts_About_NA.html (accessed June 14, 2011).

Chapter 6

1 Schaffer Library of Drug Policy, "LSD Manufacture," http://www.druglibrary.org/schaffer/dea/pubs/lsd/LSD-5.htm (accessed May 30, 2011).

2 Peter Stafford, "Chapter 1: The LSD Family," *Psychedelics Encyclopedia,* 3d ed., (Berkeley, Calif.: Ronin Publishing Inc., 1992), 62.

3 DEA Public Affairs, "LSD: The Drug," http://web.petabox.bibalex.org/web/20011116091659/www.usdoj.gov/dea/pubs/lsd/lsd-4.htm (accessed June 14, 2011).

4 Drug Control Division: Drug Charges, Drug Penalties, "Connecticut General Statutes Revised to October 1, 2001," http://vvv.state.ct.us/dcp/PDF/Penalties.pdf (accessed June 14, 2011).

Chapter 7

1 Ecstasy.org. "Empathy through Ecstasy," http://ecstasy.org/experiences/trip100.html (accessed June 14, 2011).

2 National Institute on Drug Abuse, "NIDA InfoFacts: MDMA (Ecstasy)," http://drugabuse.gov/infofacts/ecstasy.html (accessed June 14, 2011).

3 Institute for Substance Abuse Treatment Evaluation, "Club Drugs," http://www.isate.memphis.edu/clubdrugs.html (accessed June 14, 2011).

4 James Barter, *Hallucinogens* (San Diego: Lucent Books, 2002).

5 National Institute on Drug Abuse, "NIDA InfoFacts MDMA (Ecstasy)," http://www.nida.nih.gov/infofacts/ecstasy.html (accessed May 30, 2011).

6 National Drug Intelligence Center, "Intelligence Bulletin–Ketamine," http://www.justice.gov/ndic/pubs10/10255/index.htm (accessed May 30, 2011).

7 Substance Abuse and Mental Health Services Administration, "Use of Specific Hallucinogens–2006," in National Survey on Drug Use and Health Report, http://www.oas.samhsa.gov/2k8/hallucinogens/hallucinogens.htm (accessed May 30, 2011).

Glossary

abuse Inappropriate, illegal, and/or unsafe use of a substance.

acetylcholine A neurotransmitter released at autonomic synapses and neuro-muscular junctions and formed enzymatically in the tissues from choline.

addiction The quality or state of being addicted: compulsive need for and use of a habit-forming substance (such as heroin, nicotine, or alcohol) characterized by tolerance and by well-defined physiological symptoms upon withdrawal; broadly: persistent, compulsive use of a substance known by the user to be harmful.

alkaloids Any of a host of organic compounds derived from plants; many are useful as medicines.

atropine A racemic mixture of hyoscyamine obtained from any of various solanaceous plants (such as belladonna) and used especially in the form of its sulfate for its anticholinergic effects (such as pupil dilation or inhibition of smooth muscle spasms).

autonomic nervous system The part of the nervous system responsible for unconscious actions, like heart rate. It is divided into two subparts: the sympathetic, responsible for activities that excite the body such as increasing respiration, and the parasympathetic, responsible for activities that relax the body such as those that lower blood pressure.

benzodiazepine Any of a group of aromatic lipophilic amines (such as diazepam and chlordiazepoxide) used especially as tranquilizers.

central nervous system (CNS) The brain and spinal cord; sensory nerve signals are sent to the CNS and it is responsible for many bodily activities, including movement and the release of chemical signals.

club drugs Psychoactive drugs, such as ecstasy, ketamine, and methamphetamine, the use of which is associated with social gatherings at nightclubs, bars, parties, and raves.

88

delusion   A persistent false psychotic belief regarding the self or persons or objects outside the self that is maintained despite indisputable evidence to the contrary; also, the abnormal state marked by such beliefs.

dependence   A need to use a substance, despite its adverse affects on the user or those around them, in order to function normally or avoid withdrawal symptoms.

depersonalization   A psychopathological syndrome characterized by loss of identity and feelings of unreality and strangeness about one's own behavior.

designer drug   A synthetic version of a controlled substance (such as heroin) that is produced with a slightly altered molecular structure to avoid having it classified as an illicit drug.

dextromethorphan   A cough suppressant that is widely used, especially in the form of a hydrated hydrogen bromide complex.

dimenhydrinate   A crystalline antihistamine used especially to prevent nausea (such as in motion sickness).

DMT   A naturally occurring or easily synthesized hallucinogenic drug that is chemically similar to but shorter-acting than psilocybin.

dopamine   A neurotransmitter that causes euphoric feelings.

epinephrine   A neurotransmitter that stimulates striated muscle, which is under conscious control.

ergot   The black or dark purple sclerotium of fungi (genus *Claviceps*) that occurs as a club-shaped body replacing the seed of a grass (such as rye); also, a fungus bearing ergots.

euphoria   A feeling of well-being or elation.

heroin   A powerful, highly addictive narcotic made by boiling morphine; also known as diacetylmorphine.

hyperthermia   Exceptionally high fever, especially when induced artificially for therapeutic purposes.

hypothermia   Subnormal temperature of the body.

jimsonweed   A tall, poisonous, annual weed (*Datura stramonium*) of the nightshade family with rank-smelling foliage, large white or violet trumpet-shaped flowers, and roundish prickly fruit; also called thorn apple.

ketamine   A general anesthetic administered intravenously and intramuscularly in the form of its hydrochloride.

lorazepam   Benzodiazepine used especially to relieve anxiety.

lysergic acid   A crystalline acid from ergotic alkaloids.

metabolize   To perform metabolism—the sum of the processes in the buildup and destruction of protoplasm; specifically, the chemical changes in living cells by which energy is provided for vital processes and activities and new material is assimilated.

neurons   Nervous system cells with the specific job of transmitting signals to each other to coordinate a host of bodily functions.

neurotransmitters   Chemicals released by neurons to communicate with each other.

norepinephrine   A neurotransmitter that stimulates smooth muscles such as the heart and keeps blood pressure from lowering too much.

panic attack   An episode of intense fear or apprehension that is of sudden onset.

paranoia   A psychosis characterized by systematized delusions of persecution or grandeur, usually without hallucinations.

parasympathetic system   The part of the autonomic nervous system responsible for activities that relax the body such as those that lower blood pressure.

Parkinson's disease   A chronic, progressive neurological disease chiefly of later life that is linked to decreased dopamine production in the substantia nigra and is marked especially by tremor of resting muscles, rigidity, slowness of movement, impaired balance, and a shuffling gait; also called paralysis agitans, Parkinson's, Parkinson's syndrome.

peripheral nervous system   The part of the nervous system that is outside the central nervous system and comprises the cranial nerves excepting the optic nerve, the spinal nerves, and the autonomic nervous system.

phencyclidine   A piperidine derivative used chiefly in the form of its hydrochloride, especially as a veterinary anesthetic and sometimes illicitly as a psychedelic drug; also called angel dust, PCP.

pineal gland   A small, usually conical appendage in the brain of all craniate vertebrates that functions primarily as an endocrine gland secreting melatonin and that in a few reptiles has the essential structure of an eye; also called pineal, pineal body, pineal organ.

schizophrenia   A psychotic disorder characterized by loss of contact with the environment, by noticeable deterioration in the level of functioning in everyday life, and by disintegration of personality expressed as disorder of feeling, thought (such as delusions), perception (such as hallucinations), and behavior; also called *dementia praecox.*

scopolamine   A poisonous alkaloid similar to atropine that is found in various solanaceous plants and is used for its anticholinergic effects (such as preventing nausea in motion sickness and inducing mydriasis); also called hyoscine.

serotonin   A neurotransmitter that inhibits bodily activities and acts as a counter to norepinephrine.

somatic nervous system   The part of the nervous system that controls voluntary body movements via muscles and nerves.

sympathetic system   The part of the autonomic nervous system responsible for activities that excite the body, such as those that increase respiration.

synaptic cleft   The space between neurons.

thujone   A fragrant, oily ketone occurring in various essential oils—also called absinthol.

further Resources

Books

Anonymous. *Go Ask Alice. New Jersey:* Prentice Hall, 1971.
Barter, James. *Hallucinogens.* San Diego: Lucent Books, 2002.
Huxley, Aldous. *The Doors of Perception.* New York: Harper & Row, 1954.
Williams, Mary E. *Hallucinogens.* Farmington Hills, Mich.: Greenhaven Press, 2005.

Web Sites

AboveTheInfluence.com
http://www.abovetheinfluence.com

Centers for Disease Control and Prevention
http://www.cdc.gov

KidsHealth.org
http://kidshealth.org

Monitoring the Future Survey
http://monitoringthefuture.org

National Institute on Drug Abuse
http://www.nida.nih.gov/nidahome.html

NIDA for Teens
http://teens.drugabuse.gov

Office of National Drug Control Policy
http://www.whitehousedrugpolicy.gov

U.S. Drug Enforcement Administration
http://www.justice.gov/dea/

Index

About the Author

Thomas Santella currently works as an account manager at Seamless.com. Formerly, he worked as the project coordinator for the CEO and president of Lannett Company Inc., America's oldest generic pharmaceutical company. Prior to this, Santella worked as the research coordinator at the Center for Pharmaceutical Health Services Research within Temple University's School of Pharmacy. In addition to numerous articles published in peer-reviewed medical journals such as *Formulary, Pharmacy Times,* and the *Harvard Asia Pacific Review,* Santella is the author of two books in the DRUGS: THE STRAIGHT FACTS series, including *Opium* and *Body Enhancement Products.* When not working and writing in the pharmaceutical field, Santella works as a freelance food journalist and photographer. He enjoys cooking and travel and lives in Brooklyn, New York.

About the Consulting Editor

Consulting editor **David J. Triggle, Ph.D.,** is a SUNY Distinguished Professor and the University Professor at the State University of New York at Buffalo. These are the two highest academic ranks of the university. Professor Triggle received his education in the United Kingdom with a Ph.D. degree in chemistry at the University of Hull. Following post-doctoral fellowships at the University of Ottawa (Canada) and the University of London (United Kingdom) he assumed a position in the School of Pharmacy at the University at Buffalo. He served as chairman of the Department of Biochemical Pharmacology from 1971 to 1985 and as dean of the School of Pharmacy from 1985 to 1995. From 1996 to 2001 he served as dean of the Graduate School and from 1999 to 2001 was also the University Provost. He is currently the University Professor, in which capacity he teaches bioethics and science policy, and is president of the Center for Inquiry Institute, a think tank located in Amherst, New York, and devoted to issues around the public understanding of science. In the latter respect he is a major contributor to the online M.Ed. program—"Science and The Public"—in the Graduate School of Education and The Center for Inquiry.